Church of the N

Leawood, Kansas 66

Jesus' words at the Last Supper:
"I am the vine, and you are the branches."

The 2000 year-old Catholic Church,
the 150 year-old Archdiocese of Kansas City,
and the 14 year-old Nativity Parish,
all draw life from Jesus who is the vine.

All of us, as branches, are attached to
Jesus and are also attached to each other.

Because of this reality, we have so much
power for good.
Let's share it!

Fr. Al Rockers

The Archdiocese of Kansas City in Kansas

150 Years of Faith
1850 - 2000

ÉDITIONS
DU SIGNE

SPECIAL THANKS TO

Most Reverend James P. Keleher,
Archbishop of Kansas City in Kansas

Susan Carroll

The *Leaven*

Father Leo Cooper

Karen Wood

Lori Wood Habiger

Text by
Todd Habiger

Photos by
Mark ROWLANDS, Frantisek ZVARDON, and Doug HESSE
and courtesy of the Archdiocese of Kansas City in Kansas archives and *Leaven* archives

Editorial Consultant
Mary Cabrini DURKIN, OSU

Layout by
Juliette ROUSSEL

Director of Publication
Dr. Claude-Bernard COSTECALDE

Published by
Éditions du Signe
1, rue Alfred Kastler
67038 Strasbourg, Cedex 2 - France
Tel: (33) 3 88 78 91 91 / Fax: (33) 3 88 78 91 99

Publishing Director
Christian Riehl

The Archdiocese of Kansas City in Kansas
12615 Parallel Parkway / Kansas City, Kansas 66109 / 913-721-1570

© 2000 Éditions du Signe
ISBN 2-7468-0031-4
Printed in Italy by Albagraf (Pomezia)

TABLE OF CONTENTS

My dear Friends in Christ,

It is a blessed coincidence that, as the universal Catholic Church celebrates the Great Jubilee of the year 2000 and the beginning of a new millennium, the Church of the Archdiocese of Kansas City in Kansas celebrates our 150 years as a pilgrim people of faith.

In 1850 Pope Pius IX established a vicariate (a forerunner to a diocese) in Kansas to evangelize the Native Americans living in this vast area which included all of the territories of Kansas and Nebraska, Colorado up to the Rockies, and the two Dakotas. He appointed Bishop John Baptist Miege, SJ, as the first bishop. With the passage of time and because of the rapid spread of Christianity, this vicariate soon became the Diocese of Leavenworth. It became an archdiocese when the Episcopal See was transferred to Kansas City, Kansas, in 1947.

In celebrating the 150th anniversary of the creation of the first ecclesiastical jurisdiction in the United States west of St. Louis, we are reminding ourselves that the Christian faith that we can so easily take for granted was won in the face of tremendous adversities not only by the first missionaries to the Native Americans, but also at the cost of heavy hardships borne by the Catholics of that time. It was by the sweat of their brow and personal sacrifice that our ancestors built the parishes and churches which are now the glory of our archdiocese. God has favored our local Church with blessings beyond all telling! "It is right and just," therefore, "to give thanks to the Lord" for all these gracious benefits.

This commemorative history is our story of faith. Those who have gone before us were challenged to follow the way of Christ. As we recall their missionary spirit, we should be grateful for their efforts, realizing that ours is a graced moment, a spirit-filled opportunity to continue to spread the good news of salvation and share it with others.

May God bless all of you, the special people of our archdiocese, as we continue the journey and set the spirit of our Church for the next millennium.

Sincerely in Christ,

+ James P. Keleher

Most Reverend James Patrick Keleher

1

HISTORY OF
THE ARCHDIOCESE

Potawatomi are in the foreground among the different peoples depicted in this stained-glass window at Sacred Heart Church in Mound City. Jesuit priests evangelized the Potawatomi at Sugar Creek near Mound City.

NEARLY 200 YEARS AGO, a group of Jesuit priests from Maryland arrived in the area that is now Kansas and began a new life as missionaries to Native Americans. Fending off the immense dangers this untamed frontier held, these Jesuits were the creative architects of what would eventually become the Archdiocese of Kansas City in Kansas.

Thus humbly born, Catholicism in Kansas thrived, nourished by the Eucharistic blood and body of Christ in his pilgrim people and guided by the Spirit. Now, at the start of this new millennium, the Archdiocese of Kansas City in Kansas is flourishing. With 120 vibrant parishes, a school system committed to providing quality education throughout the archdiocese, a strong social service presence through Catholic Charities and special ministries, an emphasis on increased prayer and faith-sharing, and with its own commitment to missionary activities elsewhere, the future seems bright indeed.

First contact

Left:
A weather-worn statue of two Native Americans at St. Philippine Duchesne Shrine near Mound City

Soon after the discovery of the new world in the 15th century came an age of conquest and the search for riches.

Famed explorer and conqueror Francisco Coronado was intrigued by tales of Quivira, a fruitful and wealthy city said to exist north of Mexico. Organizing an expedition that included a young friar, Father Juan de Padilla, Coronado set out to find Quivira. That expedition was a failure. Coronado entered what is now Kansas in 1541 and found Quivira, but none of the tales turned out to be true. What he discovered was a group of poor Native Americans with no riches.

But where Coronado saw disappointment, Father Padilla saw opportunity. Hoping to evangelize the Native Americans, Father Padilla requested and was granted a transfer to the territory. It turned out to be a short tenure. After less than a year in the territory, Father Padilla was caught between warring tribes and killed. It would be almost 300 years before a Catholic presence was felt again in what would later become Kansas.

An undated photo of Native Americans in Kansas

Missions established

In 1823, a group of Jesuits from White Marsh, Maryland, ventured onto the frontier and established a seminary in Florissant, Missouri. Led by Father Charles Felix Van Quickenborne, the Jesuits began missionary work in Missouri, Iowa, Nebraska and Kansas. The first permanent mission established in Kansas in 1836 was among the Kickapoo located north of Leavenworth. Father Van Quickenborne also started a school there with government aid. The mission was short-lived. Most of the Kickapoo clung to their ancient customs and religion. Frustrated, in 1838 the Jesuits considered abandoning the mission, but a Kickapoo chief — Pashishi — begged them not to leave. "It is I who invited you here," he said. "I send my children to your school. You have done more good here in a year than others have done in five or six. You have cured our children of smallpox, you have befriended us in our needs, and you have been kind even to the wicked. The storm which makes the thunder roar above your heads will not last forever."

This painting at the St. Philippine Duchesne Shrine near Mound City depicts the Trail of Death.

9

These crosses at the St. Philippine Duchesne Shrine near Mound City were erected as a memorial to the more than 600 members of the Potawatomi tribe who are buried in unmarked graves near and on the site.

The Jesuits stuck with the mission. However, when the government cut off funding for the school in 1840 because of lack of students, the Jesuits finally gave up and abandoned the mission.

A sign marks the spot of St. Mary's Mission. When the Potawatomi were forced westward, the mission was burned to the ground to prevent the buildings from being desecrated.

In the late 1830s the government forced some 900 Potawatomi from their land in Indiana. Soldiers organized the Potawatomi in a single-file line more than a mile long and forced them to march more than 600 miles over three months. A priest who accompanied the Potawatomi from Indiana wrote this account at the end of one particularly difficult day: "It was a heartbreaking spectacle. Sick and dying people everywhere; almost all of the children were in a state of utter exhaustion and unconsciousness." The forced march — known as the Trail of Death — ended near present day Osawatomie and cost many Native Americans their lives.

Most of the surviving Potawatomi eventually settled in Sugar Creek near Mound City. These Potawatomi had already been exposed to Christianity and thus were more receptive to the Jesuits.

The Jesuits wasted no time opening a school for Native American boys in 1840. The Religious of the Sacred Heart were invited to join the Jesuits in their endeavor and opened a school for girls a year later. Among the Religious of the Sacred Heart who evangelized in the area was Mother Rose Philippine Duchesne, a woman destined for sainthood. Although Mother Duchesne could not speak the Potawatomi language, she made a lasting impression through her example of nursing the sick and praying. Among the Potawatomi she was known as the "woman who prays always."

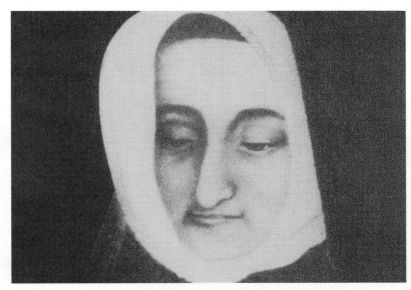

St. Philippine Duchesne's life-long dream was to serve the Native American population. She got her wish at the age of 72 when she was assigned to St. Mary's Mission.

The establishment of the Sugar Creek mission became a catalyst for missionary activity. In 1847 a highly successful mission was established among the Osage tribe near what is now St. Paul in southeast Kansas. The Jesuits started a boys' school, and the Sisters of Loretto educated the girls. Both schools were well received.

In 1847 the government made a deal that forced the Potawatomi further westward.

Before they left, however, the Potawatomi burned the Sugar Creek mission to the ground to save the buildings from desecration. They eventually settled on the banks of the Kansas River near Topeka, dubbing the mission St. Mary's. The Jesuits and the Religious Sisters of the Sacred Heart followed. A church was built and dedicated to the Immaculate Conception.

A successful mission was established in 1847 among the Osage.

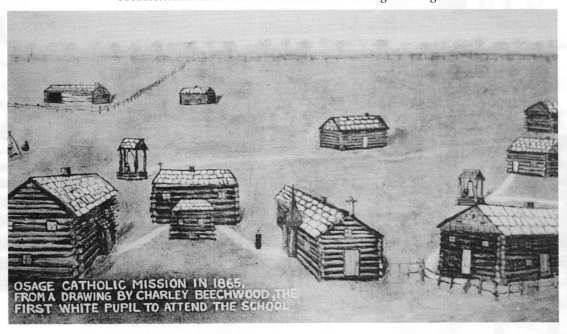

OSAGE CATHOLIC MISSION IN 1865, FROM A DRAWING BY CHARLEY BEECHWOOD, THE FIRST WHITE PUPIL TO ATTEND THE SCHOOL

St. Philippine Duchesne realized her dream of working with Native Americans at the age of 72.

FOR MOST OF HER LIFE, Mother Rose Philippine Duchesne had one desire — to work among the Native Americans.

Though this French-born nun had led an amazing life — she survived the religious persecution of the French Revolution, established the first convent of the Religious of the Sacred Heart in America in St. Charles,

Missouri, and founded many schools and orphanages — Mother Duchesne always held out hope that she would become a missionary to the Native Americans.

But those hopes seemed to have little chance of coming to fruition, as Mother Duchesne grew old and her health began to fail. Still, she asked her superiors for the opportunity even after she passed the age of 70.

Her superiors, however, were reluctant to allow Mother Duchesne to follow her dream because of her failing health and the high esteem in which others in the religious community held her. But Mother Duchesne had allies in Father Peter De Smet, SJ, and later Father Peter John Verhaegen, SJ, who were doing missionary work in Kansas. The two priests recognized Mother Duchesne's missionary zeal and begged her superiors to allow her the opportunity she had yearned for.

When Father Verhaegen secured the services of the Religious of the Sacred Heart to teach Native American girls at a mission in Sugar

This painting at the St. Philippine Duchesne Shrine near Mound City shows the saint in prayer with the Potawatomi behind her. The Potawatomi had a great love for St. Philippine Duchesne. They called her "Woman who prays always."

This marker at the St. Philippine Duchesne Shrine stands in front of a memorial to the saint.

Creek, he fully expected Mother Duchesne to be among those making the trip. When he arrived in St. Charles to escort the nuns, he was surprised to learn that that was not the case. In her book, *"Philippine Duchesne,"* Louise Callan quotes Father Verhaegen as saying to Mother Duchesne's superior, "But she must come, too. Even if she can use only one leg, she will come. Why, if we have to carry her all the way on our shoulders, she is coming with us. She may not be able to do much work, but she will assure success to the mission by praying for us. Her very presence will draw down all manner of heavenly favors on the work."

The point was well taken. Mother Duchesne, despite her poor health, was finally getting her chance to become a missionary to the Native Americans. She was 72 years old. The trip to Sugar Creek revitalized Mother Duchesne, and her health seemed to improve. When the entourage of Father Verhaegen, Mother Duchesne and three other nuns arrived at the Sugar Creek mission, they were greeted by 700 members of the Potawatomi tribe.

Mother Duchesne's time among the Potawatomi was difficult. Her health once again began to deteriorate and she had a constant fever. Yet she attended Mass daily. Even during the depth of winter she made her way through the snow to the unheated church.

Making matters even more difficult was the fact that she was never able to master the Potawatomi language as the other Sisters had. She was depressed about her lack of comprehension of the language, and the fact that she was of little help. Her major contributions were to visit the sick and help the Native American girls with their knitting.

Nevertheless, she was revered by the Potawatomi. They called her "Woman who prays always." It has been said that she spent eight hours a day in prayer. Often, the Potawatomi would quietly slip into the church as Mother Duchesne prayed, and would kiss the hem of her habit.

Finally, after only a year at the Sugar Creek mission, Mother Duchesne was summoned back to St. Charles. When Father Verhaegen was informed of the order, he dropped his other missionary activities and returned to Sugar Creek. He had escorted Mother Duchesne safely to the mission, and he would take her back to St. Charles, although it pained him greatly to do so. They left the mission on June 19, 1842.

Mother Duchesne spent the remainder of her life in St. Charles, where she died on Nov. 18, 1852. She was canonized in 1988.

The stained-glass windows at Sacred Heart Church in Mound City show several scenes from the life of St. Philippine Duchesne, including her work with the Potawatomi.

THE VICARIATE APOSTOLIC

While the missions among the Osage and Potawatomi proved successful, little missionary work had been done in the vast Indian Territory established by the government in 1832.

In 1849, the Catholic Church decided that a more vigorous missionary effort to the Native Americans was needed. Thus in 1850 Pope Pius IX established the Vicariate Apostolic East of the Rocky Mountains. A vicariate apostolic is a territorial division of the church that does not have the full status of a diocese. The vast territory, comprised of more than one million square miles, stretched from the Missouri River to the Rockies and from Canada to Texas.

A young Jesuit priest, just three years ordained, was chosen to lead the vicariate. It was an assignment Father John Baptist Miege did not want.

The Vicariate Apostolic East of the Rocky Mountains, established in 1850, comprised what is now Kansas, Nebraska, Oklahoma, North Dakota, South Dakota, and parts of Colorado and Wyoming.

BISHOP JOHN BAPTIST MIEGE, SJ

Bishop Miege was the first bishop of the Vicariate Apostolic East of the Rocky Mountains.

John Baptist Miege was born in 1815 in France. He entered the Society of Jesus in 1836 and was ordained to the priesthood in 1847. A year later he was granted permission to serve the missions in North America, eventually finding himself in St. Louis.

Because of his youth and lack of self-confidence, Father Miege at first declined the assignment to lead the vicariate.

In his book, *Bishop East of the Rockies: The Life and Letters of John Baptist Miege, S.J.*, author Herman J. Muller, SJ, quotes a letter from Father Miege to his brother Urban explaining his reluctance to accept the position. It says in part, "I would a thousand times rather return to Europe than accept this dignity. I have enough difficulty keeping myself out of trouble when I have only myself to guide, what would it be if I had to guide others?"

Nevertheless, Father Miege's superior, Father Druyts, ordered him to accept the position. Father Druyts told Father Miege that he was about to take charge of the "strangest diocese in the world." He was consecrated a bishop on March 25, 1851, in St. Louis.

A chalice which belonged to Bishop Miege, now preserved by the Sisters of Charity of Leavenworth.

14

The church compound, located in St. Marys, served as Bishop Miege's home for four years.

When the Kansas territory was opened up to white settlement, Leavenworth exploded and became a center of activity in Kansas.

A month later, accompanied by Jesuit Father Paul Ponziglione, Bishop Miege made his way to the St. Mary's mission where he set up his residence. Immediately the young bishop went to work teaching catechism, preaching, visiting the sick and administering the sacraments.

WHITE SETTLERS ARRIVE

In 1854, the federal government passed the Kansas-Nebraska Act, which established the territories of Kansas and Nebraska in the former Indian Territory and opened it up to white settlement. The act also gave each territory the right to determine the question of slavery for itself.

Bishop Miege saw this as a death sentence for the Native Americans. Still, he realized that he had an obligation to the incoming

Many early settlers in Kansas lived in sod houses like this and struggled for survival on the plains.

An early settler in Kansas collects a wheelbarrow full of manure from the Kansas plain.

white settlers as well as the Native Americans. Realizing that there would be growth along the Missouri River, the bishop moved his residence to Leavenworth. He formally established the Cathedral of the Immaculate Conception on August 15, 1855.

Growth was rapid in eastern Kansas as both pro- and anti-slavery supporters rushed to the area in hopes of influencing the slavery decision. Just as Bishop Miege had predicted, settlements were developed all along the river banks. In all, 25 parishes were established between 1855 and 1861. The Kansas territory had the reputation of being a lawless land. Conflicts between pro- and anti-slavery factions were commonplace. Bishop Miege was so fearful of the situation that he took to sleeping with a gun close at hand. One night the bishop was awakened by a sound and ended up shooting the tail off a nearby pig. That ended the bishop's association with firearms.

A 610-square-foot fresco entitled *The Trinity and Episodes of Benedictine Life* by Jean Carlot hangs in St. Benedict's Abbey. This portion of the fresco represents the monks' first educational efforts in Atchison.

THE BENEDICTINE MONKS

To serve the area's increasing population, Bishop Miege put out a call for more priests and religious to complement the meager group of diocesan priests.

Benedictine Father Henry Lemke was one of the first to answer the call. Father Lemke came from Pennsylvania in 1855 with the intent of establishing an abbey in Kansas. He eventually settled in Doniphan where he built a small church and enlisted the help of

Father Augustine Wirth and the not-yet-ordained Casimir Seitz. On April 26, 1857, Seitz became the first priest ordained in Kansas by Bishop Miege. Soon thereafter Father Lemke left the area to return to Pennsylvania, leaving Father Wirth, who moved to Atchison and established a Benedictine monastery there in 1858. The Benedictines were instrumental in shaping Catholicism in the northeast corner of Kansas. They developed missionary circuits near the abbey and along the Missouri River. By 1860 they were caring for 23 mission stations.

The life of these early circuit priests was not easy. It required inner strength and dedication. In a letter, Father Wirth recounted the experience this way: "With an entire chapel in a traveling bag, which is tossed on the horse's back, the priest wanders from one station to another, the family table serving as an altar... . The houses in which people live do not deserved that name; they are ordinarily of one room, sixteen feet square, that also serves as the kitchen. In this room there are one or two beds, a table and a stove, so the room is already full, and here in the midst of a crowd the priest must also sleep, which is very unpleasant. The houses are so badly built that the wind whistles in from all sides, so that it is a wonder that the people do not get sick and die."

Despite the hardships, many Catholic communities were established, nurtured and encouraged in northeast Kansas. The bond that developed well over 100 years ago continues today as the Benedictine Fathers are still responsible for much of the pastoral care in northeast Kansas.

St. Bede Parish in Kelly is one of the many churches served by the Benedictines.

THE BENEDICTINE SISTERS

The Benedictine Sisters were quick to begin their own efforts in Kansas. Seven nuns, led by their prioress, Mother Evangelista Kremmeter, arrived in Atchsion in 1863, responding to the need for teachers. A convent was provided for them, although the debt had not been paid off. Legend has it that shortly after their arrival, close to 100 local families began contributing 50 cents a month to pay off the debt. Within three weeks of arriving, the Sisters opened a school. That school would eventually evolve into Benedictine College.

In 1876, the Benedictine Sisters began their long history of staffing parish schools, starting with Sts. Peter and Paul School in Seneca. Their educational influence has been far-reaching over the years, as the Sisters have taught in more than 125 schools in the four-state area of Kansas, Nebraska, Iowa and Missouri during their long history.

St. Scholastica is the patron of Benedictine women's monasteries.

SISTERS OF CHARITY

While attending the provincial council of 1858 in St. Louis, Bishop Miege had a chance encounter with Mother Xavier Ross, a Sister of Charity from Nashville.
The Sisters of Charity had had a falling out with the bishop of Nashville and were searching for a new home. At the same time, Bishop Miege had a desperate need for teachers. It was a perfect match.

Mother Xavier Ross brought the Sisters of Charity from Nashville to Leavenworth in 1858.

Sister Catherine Labouré Conway enjoys a quite moment of prayer at the Sisters of Charity motherhouse in Leavenworth.

The Sisters of Charity of Leavenworth arrived in 1858 and established a convent.

Mother Xavier brought five Sisters, one novice, two postulants and an orphan girl to Leavenworth in November, 1858. They began teaching immediately. For Catholics not living in the Leavenworth area, the order established a girls' boarding school, which opened in the spring of 1860. In 1923, the Sisters established Saint Mary College. Bishop Miege realized what good fortune he had in the Sisters of Charity and did everything he could to accommodate them. In 1859 he helped them establish a

novitiate. Although there were few candidates at first, the community could count 27 professed religious within six years.

A few years after their arrival, the Sisters established a hospital — St. John's — in 1864. The establishment of the hospital was a foreshadowing of things to come. From 1864 to 1952 the Sisters of Charity established or assumed responsibility for 18 hospitals from Kansas to California. In 1972, they formed the Sisters of Charity of Leavenworth Health Services Corporation (SCL/HSC) a not-for-profit corporation. The SCL/HSC has become a major player in health care. It currently owns four clinics and 10 hospitals in the United States.

THE CARMELITES

The sun shines high above St. Boniface Church in Scipio, one of the first churches in Kansas staffed by Carmelite priests.

In 1864, two Carmelite priests, Fathers Cyril Knoll and Xavier Huber, arrived in Leavenworth from Europe and were immediately given

Saint Mary College in Leavenworth was established by the Sisters of Charity of Leavenworth in 1923.

responsibility for St. Joseph Parish by Bishop Miege. St. Joseph was the first permanent foundation of the Carmelites in America. They were later joined by Father Theodore Heimann, Bishop Miege's vicar general, and the recently ordained Father Louis Guenther, both of whom applied for admission to the Order of Carmel. Because of the desperate need for priests, Father Guenther — who was still just a novice — was assigned to St. Boniface Parish in Scipio in 1865. Shortly thereafter, Father Heimann joined him.

Father Heimann was an ambitious priest who in 1872 decided to build a monastery and a larger church in Scipio, with the help of generous contributions from his friends. Not content with just a monastery and church, Father Heimann decided to open a college in 1873. The college was plagued by staffing problems and debt almost immediately and lasted only a short time.

Even today, more than 100 years after they first arrived in the area, the Carmelites remain fixtures as pastors of parishes in Scipio, Richmond and Leavenworth.

. Joseph Church, Leavenworth, has long en staffed by Carmelite priests.

Left: **The virgin land in Kansas made plowing ifficult for early settlers.**

Right: **A woman does her part to make a life in Kansas.**

POPULATION BOOM

The post-Civil War years saw the state's population accelerate considerably. The Homestead Act, which granted 160 acres of land to each settler, was one of the reasons. Many of these early settlers, lured by cheap land, came to Kansas with little money but great hopes for a better life. Most were not prepared for what they encountered. The virgin land in Kansas was difficult to break, thus making the initial plowing expensive and labor intensive. The early part of the 1860s also saw severe winters and drought which led to crop failures.

Railroad construction also contributed to Kansas' growth spurt. Between 1860 and 1870, the population more than tripled, going from 107,206 to 364,399.

With this population boom, the church in Kansas began to expand. With railroads making travel easier, parishes were being established all over the state in places never before imaginable. Along with these new parishes came parochial schools, as many of the pioneering priests felt faith and education went hand in hand.

These early parishes were poor and Mass was said in private homes simply because people had to put all their resources into their land to ensure survival.

As Father Wirth wrote: "The settler … needs all the money that he brings with him, and the best will in the world can do little or nothing for the church and school. It is three

or four years before he can spare something."

Many of the settlers who came to Kansas in search of cheap land found it at quite a distance from the main settlements and thus isolated from faith centers, often hundreds of miles

Woodcut of St. Isidore, patron saint of farmers - St. Louis Church, Good Intent.

The construction of railroads contributed to the population boom in Kansas between 1860 and 1870.

The early part of the 1860s saw drought and crop failures, unlike this modern crop which flourished in 1999.

away. Bishop Miege was troubled by this, feeling that many Catholics were losing, or in danger of losing their faith. In his book *The Catholic Church on the Kansas Frontier*, Father Peter Beckman, OSB, quotes a 1859 letter from Bishop Miege to a friend: "The number of lost sheep cannot be counted; and the evil will increase daily unless our Lord sends me true laborers in his vineyard."

This was a legitimate concern, one that Bishop Miege never found a complete solution for. Despite that fact, the church in Kansas continued to grow. By 1869, there were 55 churches scattered throughout Kansas. There were also 82 missions without churches, which were visited by priests from time to time.

BISHOP MIEGE RESIGNS

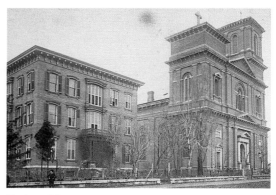

Bishop Miege tried to resign as bishop of the vicariate in 1869, but his resignation was refused because of the large debt on the cathedral.

In 1869, Bishop Miege requested, and was granted, the appointment of Benedictine Father Louis Fink — the prior of the Benedictines in Atchison — to be his coadjutor bishop. Bishop Fink's poor health at the time of his consecration caused one bishop to call it "a waste of holy oils."

That same year during a trip to Rome, Bishop Miege asked to be relieved of his duties, citing poor health and a desire to prepare for death. His request fell upon deaf ears, mostly because of the large debt of the cathedral in Leavenworth.

After fundraising efforts in Leavenworth failed, Bishop Miege set off for South America near the end of 1871 in an attempt to raise the money to pay the debt, leaving the vicariate to the care of Bishop Fink.

After two-and-a-half years braving the terrain of South America, Bishop Miege returned to Leavenworth having raised approximately $42,000: half the debt on the cathedral. Soon thereafter his resignation was accepted in 1874.

Bishop Miege quietly slipped away from Leavenworth, leaving behind for his priests only a note which read, "When you will receive this note I shall be far away. Thank you for all your kindness to me and pray for me. J.B. Miege."

After months of rest at St. Louis University, Bishop Miege went to Woodstock University in Maryland to give spiritual direction to students and aspiring missionaries. In 1877, he left Woodstock and helped found Detroit College and served as its first president. Bishop Miege left Detroit in 1880 to return to Woodstock, which he loved dearly. He died there on August 3, 1884.

BISHOP FINK TAKES OVER

By the time Bishop Miege's resignation was accepted in 1874, Bishop Fink was more than familiar with the church in Kansas, having assumed most of its responsibilities during Bishop Miege's absence.

To many the year 1874 was known as the year of the grasshopper. In late summer a plague of grasshoppers invaded the state, annihilating nearly all vegetation in its path.

The state board of agriculture reported that "the air was filled and the fields and trees were completely covered with these voracious trespassers. At one time the total destruction of every green thing seemed imminent."

Bishop Louis Fink was the second bishop in Kansas.

St. Patrick Church in Atchison is the oldest church still in use in Kansas. It was built in 1866 and shows the wear of its years.

The cornerstone of Assumption Church in Topeka with the capitol building in the background. The parish dates back to 1862.

In the book *Heritage of Kansas,* edited by Everett Rich, Anne E. Bingham remembered the plague this way: "One afternoon in August as I sat sewing I heard a noise on the roof like hailstones. Stepping out I saw the air full of grasshoppers.... They got down to business right away.... The sides of the house and the walks were covered with them. They flew up like a swarm of bees at one's step. They had the most voracious appetites of any living thing. One or two would begin on a melon; as the place grew larger others came, and the melon would soon be eaten down to the shell."

Bishop Fink feared that many would starve as a result of the disaster, but the state recovered surprisingly quickly.

Bishop Fink was an effective organizer. He sent pastoral instructions to priests advising them how to administer parishes efficiently, as well as communicating his desires about Lenten regulations and fundraising. Bishop Fink also stressed the importance of involving the laity in the decision-making process of the parish. He required that each parish form a committee and hold committee meetings once a month in parishes and once every three months in missions. These committees were intended to keep order in the parish, discuss building projects with the pastor and assist with weekly collections.

Sts. Cyril and Methodius in Kansas City, Kansas, was an ethnic parish that served the Slovaks.

Bishop Fink's mandates were considered revolutionary at the time and were not met with great enthusiasm by many priests who resented the bishop's "interference."

While Bishop Miege had requested that Kansas be elevated to diocesan status some years earlier, Bishop Fink presented a compelling case to the Holy See, pointing out that of the 58 dioceses in the United States, only 30 had more priests, parishioners and churches than his vicariate. At the time of his report, there were 45,000 Catholics, 60 priests, 80 churches and chapels, an abbey, seven colleges, 20 parochial schools, an orphanage and a hospital.

The point was well taken and on May 22, 1877, the vicariate was elevated to diocesan status. Ten years later the state was divided into three dioceses with sees in Leavenworth, Wichita and Concordia (now Salina).

THE RISE OF ETHNIC PARISHES

Bishop Fink was an avid promoter of Kansas. He advertised in newspapers in the United States and Europe, promising stable Catholic communities to new arrivals. And immigrants responded.

In the late 1800s, many German settlers entered Kansas, settling in places such as Leavenworth, Topeka and Westphalia. In Leavenworth, Holy Epiphany Parish was established in 1874 as the first African American parish west of St. Louis.

In the Kansas City area, ethnic parishes multiplied at a tremendous rate. There were the Polish in St. Joseph Parish, the Croatians at St. John the Baptist, the Slovaks at Sts. Cyril and Methodius, the Slovenians at Holy Family, the Lithuanians at St. Casimir, the Irish at St. Mary and the Germans at St. Anthony.

Likewise many rural parishes tended to have a distinct ethnicity since nationalities often settled together. Hispanic parishes also grew during the early 1900s as many Mexicans were driven from their homeland during the Mexican Revolution, which lasted from 1910 to 1940. Hispanic families settled in Topeka, Emporia, Kansas City, Atchison and Ottawa.

These ethnic parishes incorporated native language and customs into the faith life of the parish. Strong ethnic communities formed and lasted for generations. Most of the afore-mentioned parishes still retain a strong ethnic flavor as can be seen in parish celebrations and in the Mass itself.

A statue of Blessed Juan Diego in Our Lady of Guadalupe Church in Topeka. Our Lady of Guadalupe is a Hispanic parish established after the turn of the century.

THE FRANCISCANS

While he was busy promoting Kansas, Bishop Fink was also busy recruiting religious to work in the diocese. Bishop Fink wanted as many religious as possible in the state. His hope was that strategically placed religious communities would become centers of Catholic life.

The Franciscan Fathers from the Cincinnati Province responded to Bishop Fink's plea for religious assistance in Kansas. Arriving in 1878, the Franciscans assumed responsibility for parishes in and around Emporia and Kansas City, Kansas.

At the turn of the century, as Hispanics began to arrive in Emporia, they found a friend in Franciscan Father Berthold Stauback, pastor of Sacred Heart Parish. Despite not knowing their language, he worked to fulfill their spiritual needs. In 1923, the Hispanics built a small chapel of their own and dedicated it to St. Catherine of Alexandria. St. Catherine was also cared for by the Franciscans.

In 1924, the Franciscans received a commission to establish a parish for African-Americans in Kansas City, Kansas. Named Our Lady of Perpetual Help and led by Franciscan Father Angelus Schaefer, Our Lady was an active African American parish until 1968, when it merged with St. Rose Parish to become Our Lady and St. Rose. After a long history in the archdiocese, the Franciscans left in 1993 to return to Cincinnati.

Sacred Heart Church in Emporia welcomed the Hispanics at the turn of the century.

This crucifix stands outside St. Catherine Church in Emporia. In 1923 Hispanic Catholics established St. Catherine.

Citing declining numbers of Franciscans and the distance between Kansas City, Kansas, and Cincinnati, the Franciscans returned pastorates in Emporia, Kansas City, Kansas, Hartford, Reading and Olpe to the archdiocese.

At the farewell Mass at Sacred Heart in Emporia, the provincial of St. John the Baptist Province in Cincinnati, Father John Bok, said that the decision to leave the archdiocese was a difficult, but necessary one. "You have helped the Franciscans grow in their love of God, and we thank you for that from the bottom of our hearts. You have touched our lives, and we will miss you," he said.

A worshiper holds a toddler at the 75th-anniversary celebration of the founding of Our Lady of Perpetual Help Parish in Kansas City, Kansas, in 1999. Our Lady of Perpetual Help was established by the Franciscans in 1924 with African American Catholics. Although it is no longer a parish, having merged with St. Rose Parish in 1968, Our Lady's spirit still lives on through those who were — and still consider themselves — Our Lady of Perpetual Help parishioners.

FINK AND EDUCATION

With more and more parishes being firmly established, Bishop Fink turned his attention to education. The bishop encouraged the establishment of Catholic schools, since he had a distrust of secular education, calling public schools "breeding places for godlessness and indifferentism." It was Bishop Fink's desire that a school be established in places where there were 25 or more children. Because of the poverty of many early parishes, these schools were often makeshift rooms taught by lay people or the pastor. However, as parishes grew and became more financially secure, most schools were turned over to the communities of women religious in the area.

Bishop Fink was a strong supporter of Catholics schools. He called public schools "breeding places for godlessness and indifferentism."

THE URSULINES

In 1895, the Bishop Fink invited the Ursuline Sisters to establish a school and locate their motherhouse in the diocese. They first arrived at St. Boniface Parish in Scipio to teach before settling in Paola in 1896. The Ursuline Academy, a girls' boarding school, opened March 1, 1896. In 1924, the Ursulines expanded their educational interests and added a junior college. The academy lasted for 75 years, closing in 1971.

The first Ursuline Convent building.

In the late 1960s the Ursulines were working with the mentally retarded and were instrumental in establishing Lakemary Center in Paola, a school for developmentally disabled children. "To have shared the triumph of a child who, challenged beyond belief, has learned to hold a pencil, to button his shirt, to speak a sentence or to write his name, is indescribable," Sister Rita Redmond, who worked at Lakemary, wrote in 1995.

The Ursulines continue to make an impact in Paola and the surrounding areas through their social justice and community work as well as their continuing commitment to education.

Two Ursuline Sisters care for flowers in the Lourdes shrine.

THE CAPUCHINS

In 1877, Bishop Fink invited the Capuchins to the diocese to minister to the German-speaking immigrants who had arrived in Rush and Ellis Counties in western Kansas. They established a friary in Victoria and began ministering to parishes clear to the Colorado border.

With the establishment of two new dioceses in Kansas, the Capuchins were no longer connected to the Diocese of Leavenworth. Almost a century later the Capuchins would renew their connection to the now-Archdiocese of Kansas City in Kansas. At the invitation of Archbishop Ignatius Strecker, the Capuchins returned in 1972 to help establish Good Shepherd Parish, Shawnee. In 1986 they

The Capuchins took over the pastoral care of St. John the Evangelist Parish in Lawrence in 1986.

The Capuchins established St. Conrad's Friary in Lawrence in 1986.

established St. Conrad's Friary in Lawrence and are responsible for the pastoral care of St. John the Evangelist Parish, and the Haskell Campus Center, both in Lawrence.

Early in 1904 Bishop Fink died. Before his death, he had expressed a desire to be buried in the cemetery at the Sisters of Charity motherhouse in Leavenworth. Mother Mary Regis wrote to her fellow Sisters, "He was close to us in life, will be ours in death, and I feel will be interested in us in Heaven." Bishop Fink left a lasting legacy. During the 30 years of his episcopate he established 52 new parishes — many due to his enthusiastic promotion of Kansas.

In his book *The History of Our Cradle Land,* Msgr. Thomas Kinsella wrote, "Bishop Fink was successful in obtaining for his vast diocese … a very efficient body of young priests, and as a consequence, Leavenworth became one of the best organized dioceses in the west." Bishop Fink was definitely not "a waste of holy oils."

Right: **Annunciation Parish in Frankfort was one of the many parishes established during Bishop Fink's tenure as Bishop of Leavenworth.**

The bell tower at St. Teresa Church in Westphalia overlooks the city water tower. Westphalia was established by German settlers in 1880, when Bishop Fink was promoting Kansas life in newspapers in the United States and Europe.

The Resurrection - St. Bede Church, Kelly

ALTHOUGH ITS ORIGINS are lost somewhere in the shadows of history, stained glass has become an integral part of church architecture over the centuries.

Stained-glass windows began appearing in the great cathedrals of Europe in the 10th century. The windows, especially those depicting Biblical stories, were a major vehicle of artistic expression and of religious education during the Gothic Period. Light passing through them illuminates their brilliant colors and communicates the spiritual lessons that they depict. With seemingly universal and eternal appeal, stained-glass windows have withstood the test of time and enrich churches worldwide. Many parishes in the Archdiocese of Kansas City in Kansas house beautiful and unique stained-glass windows, depicting biblical scenes, saints, miracles, the sacraments, and the history of the Church in Kansas.

The windows of Blessed Sacrament in Kansas City, Kansas, show 20th-century men and women taking part in key moments in Christ's life.

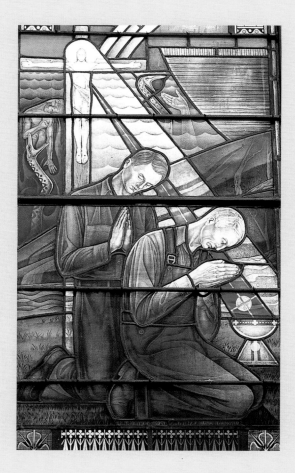

28

Three of the eight Beatitudes are seen in these windows of Christ the King Church in Kansas City, Kansas.

Angel-Abbot's chapel on the third floor of St. Benedict's Abbey.

St. Michael the Archangel - Holy Family Church, Kansas City, Kansas.

Bishop Thomas Lillis

BISHOP THOMAS LILLIS

The vicar general of the neighboring Kansas City, Missouri, Diocese, Bishop Thomas Lillis, was the successor to Bishop Fink.

Bishop Lillis arrived during a time of building. Small churches were being replaced by larger, more permanent structures. Schools, convents and rectories were also being constructed.

Amid this construction boom, Bishop Lillis saw the need to deepen the Church's role in education. He established a Catholic high school in Kansas City, Kansas, and encouraged the Sisters of Charity to begin the process of educating the local teenagers of Leavenworth, eventually culminating in the establishment of Immaculata High School.

In 1910, Bishop Lillis was appointed coadjutor bishop of the Kansas City, Missouri, Diocese. He continued to administer the Leavenworth Diocese until Bishop John Ward's consecration in 1911.

BISHOP WARD, AN EDUCATOR

Bishop Ward has the distinction of being the only native priest to be named bishop of the diocese. Following the example of his predecessors, Bishop Ward emphasized Catholic education.

Because of Bishop Ward's desire to provide Catholic education in the capital city, Topeka,

Bishop John Ward is the only native priest to have been named bishop for the Diocese of Leavenworth.

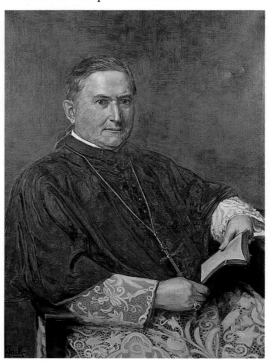

A World War I parade in 1917

Assumption High School — now Hayden — was started. Sts. Peter and Paul High School in Seneca had its origins under Bishop Ward, and Immaculata High School in Leavenworth was built.

During this time, Catholic education flourished, thanks in large part to the Benedictines, the Sisters of Charity and the Ursulines, who staffed most of the schools in the diocese.

World War I had an impact on the diocese during Bishop Ward's tenure. Anti-German sentiment was so prevalent that anything German, even German-language sermons might be considered un-American. Abbot Innocent Wolf of St. Benedict's Abbey was deeply troubled by World War I. The abbot had lived his entire life in the United States but had a strong German upbringing and blamed the war on the British. Still, the abbot understood the implications of being pro-German and the damage it might do the abbey and, especially, St. Benedict's College. When two monks began voicing their pro-German stance, Abbot Innocent took action and issued the following statement: "Remarks must not be made before students or visitors about the president, about the war, about laws made by Congress in regard to the war, about politics. If one of the community would be interned or arrested because of his remarks all will suffer and the College may even be closed. There is a motion before Congress, that the president appoint a day of prayer for the success of our army. If that passes, be absolutely sure that you say no word about it, and that your actions may not be reported as a disapproval. Let everyone sign this to show that they will obey the will of Father Abbot in a very serious matter."

Also amid the World War I hysteria, St. Bede Church in Kelly was raided by a U.S. Marshall in search of guns. After searching every corner of the church, the Marshall left, satisfied that there were no guns on the premises. The war also brought a halt to much of the migration from Europe because of strict immigration laws.

MORE RELIGIOUS ARRIVE

The Sisters Servants of Mary were brought to the diocese by industrialist Lee Sedgwick, who had witnessed their work first-hand during a trip to Puerto Rico in 1917. Upon his return to the United States, Sedgwick stopped in New Orleans, where the Sisters had a convent, and persuaded them to come to Kansas City, Kansas. With the approval of Bishop Ward, the Sisters came and began their mission to care for the sick in their homes. In 1926, a convent was provided for them, which became their provincial motherhouse for the United States and Mexico.

In 1923, the Order of Augustinian Recollects, a Spanish community of men who had come to the United States in 1914,

Sister Gabriella Fernandez, a Sister Servant of Mary, prays in the Sisters' chapel. The Sister Servants of Mary provide health care in the Kansas City metro area.

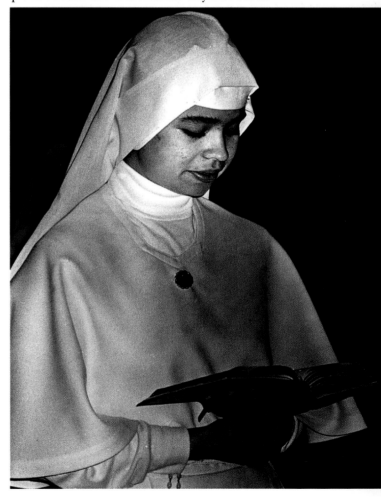

was asked to provide priestly service to the Hispanic communities in Topeka and Kansas City, taking over Our Lady of Guadalupe Parish, Topeka, and now-closed Mount Carmel Parish, Kansas City, Kansas. Ministry to Hispanics increased in 1937 with the establishment of St. John the Divine Parish, Kansas City, Kansas, which became a mission of Mount Carmel. When Mount Carmel was destroyed by the flood of 1951, St. John the Divine became the center for Hispanic spirituality in Kansas City, Kansas. After more than 60 years of Hispanic ministry in the archdiocese, the Augustinian monastery was closed in 1984.

Despite being handcuffed financially because of the Great Depression, Bishop Johannes was able to raise the funds to build Bishop Ward High School.

BISHOP FRANCIS JOHANNES

In 1928, Father Francis Johannes from St. Joseph, Missouri, was appointed as coadjutor bishop to Bishop Ward. Raised a "city boy," Bishop Johannes requested a parish assignment in a rural area. He was promptly assigned to St. Gregory Parish in Marysville where he stayed until Bishop Ward's death the following year.

Bishop Johannes inherited a diocese which had 103 parishes, 25 missions, 210 priests, 69 grade schools, 14 high schools, and seven Catholic hospitals. He also had the

unenviable fortune of inheriting the diocese at the beginning of the Great Depression.

As a direct result of the Depression, no new parishes were established during Bishop Johannes' tenure, and building programs were curtailed throughout the diocese.

With the building lull, Bishop Johannes took the opportunity to establish and nurture several lay organizations. He established the first council of the St. Vincent de Paul Society in the diocese. This group became indispensable during the depression as it worked to provide the poor throughout the diocese with basic necessities to survive this difficult time.

A further example of the growing lay involvement in the church was the establishment of the Daughters of Isabella, Knights of Columbus and the Knights and Ladies of Peter Claver.

Although building projects were severely curtailed during Bishop Johannes' tenure, he was able to raise the funds for a new Catholic high school in Kansas City, Kansas. Before his death, Bishop Ward had secured a piece of land on 18th Street. Bishop Johannes followed through on the project and dedicated Bishop Ward High School on Oct. 11, 1931.

Bishop Francis Johannes was praised for leading the diocese through the Great Depression.

On March 13, 1937, Bishop Johannes died in a hospital in Denver. He had been troubled by bronchial and heart problems for years. Upon his death, *The Kansas City Star* praised the bishop's sound business decisions which saw the Leavenworth Diocese through the Great Depression. An editorial said, "He not only saved the diocese from disintegration, but strengthened and extended the existing institutions."

BISHOP PAUL SCHULTE

Bishop Paul Schulte focused much of his effort on religious education.

With the death of Bishop Johannes, Bishop Paul Schulte of St. Louis was named to lead the Leavenworth Diocese. Although he was bishop of Leavenworth for just nine years, he made a huge impact on the spiritual development of the people of the diocese. Bishop Schulte's main thrust was religious education. It was a multidimensional effort aimed at all ages in every part of the diocese. Bishop Schulte established the Confraternity of Christian Doctrine (CCD), which was designed especially for Catholics attending public schools, and created a comprehensive plan for religious education. The program called for weekly religion classes for students attending public schools and summer vacation schools in rural areas. The bishop also encouraged street preaching by priests in areas where the Catholic presence was minimal. Priests would often descend upon a town during the summer to preach a series of lectures on the truths of Catholicism. In addition, the bishop advocated discussion groups and a religion-by-mail course which began in 1940 through St. Benedict's College in Atchison and Saint Mary College in Leavenworth.

In order to provide regular information to individuals, Bishop Schulte established a diocesan newspaper, *The Eastern Kansas Register,* in 1939. "We have long felt the need of a medium by which we could give our people the reliable Catholic news — international, national and local — as well as our own personal messages of pastoral import," the bishop wrote in the premiere issue of the *Register.* The bishop was a strong supporter of the newspaper and made it a goal to have a *Register* in every Catholic home. The *Register* became *The Leaven* in 1979. It goes to every registered Catholic home.

The premiere edition of the Eastern Kansas *Register* in 1939. *The Register* became *The Leaven* in 1979.

Father Joseph Biehler was one of many priests who engaged in street preaching in towns with no Catholic church. Bishop Schulte encouraged street preaching to help educate people on the Catholic faith and to spread the Gospel.

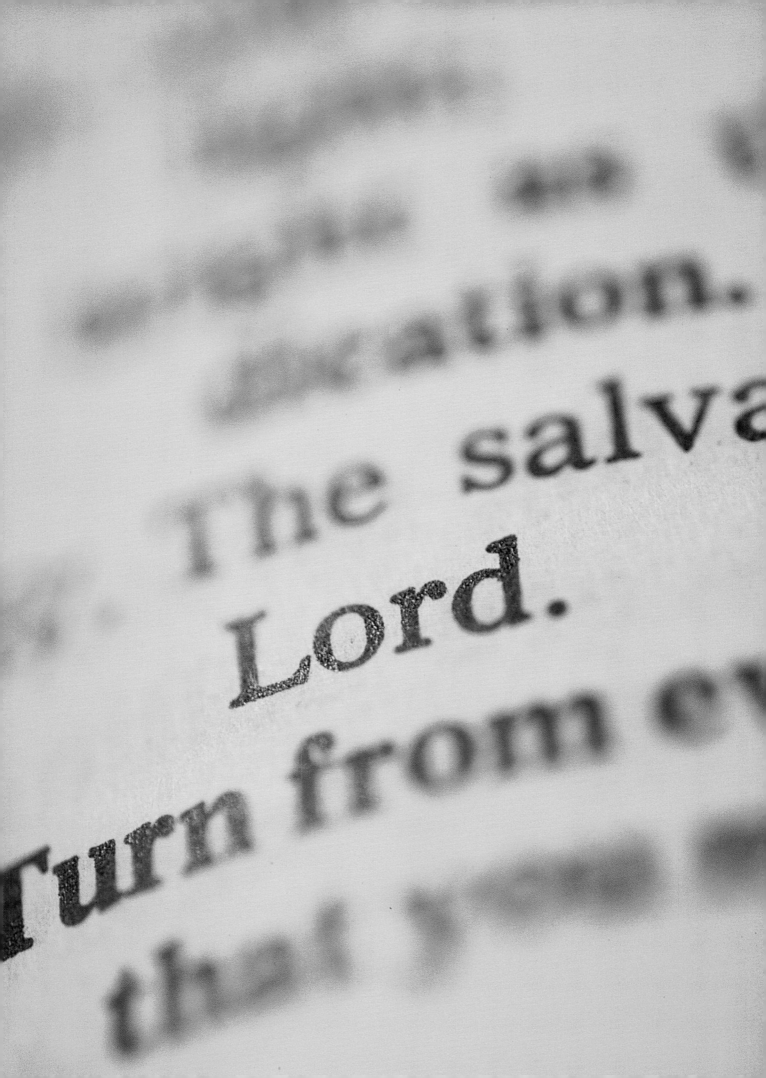

Devotional candles - St. Agnes Church in
Roeland Park

YOUTH WORK DEVELOPS

As a result of Bishop Schulte's emphasis on religious education, several youth organizations sprang to life. Father Herman Koch was the first youth director of the diocese, and under his leadership the Catholic Youth Organization developed. CYO activities began to appear in Kansas City, Kansas, Leavenworth, Atchison and Topeka. CYO recreation centers opened in Atchison and Leavenworth.

WORLD WAR II

At the time of Bishop Schulte's installation as Bishop of Leavenworth in 1937, events were unfolding in Europe and Japan that would lead to the second world war. In a matter of years the United States would be pulled into the conflict.

During this time, Bishop Schulte joined his fellow bishops in advocating peace. In a Christmas appeal in 1942, Bishop Schulte wrote: "A suggestion of peace seems strangely out of place this year, when the whole world is at war, when our soldiers are coloring the ground of every continent with their blood. It will almost seem a mockery to greet one with, 'Peace be with you,' when vacant chairs at Christmas dinners throughout the land — some 4,000 in our own little diocese — will remind fathers and mothers and sisters and brothers that their own loved ones are keeping watch with death. Can there be peace? Not peace between our nations this year, for that peace must yet be won. But another peace, that which Christ came to bring, can be ours even in the turmoil of war. And that is the true message of Christmas."

Christ's pierced feet - St. Francis Xavier Church in Burlington

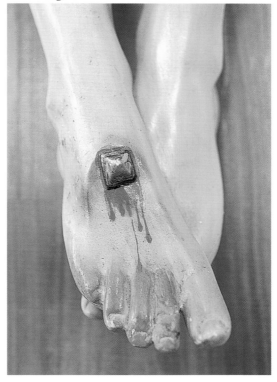

Left: **Words of Scripture - St. Pius X Church in Mission**

A crucifix stands in the background - St. Ann Church in Hiawatha.

In Emporia, a Catholic Club for boys was formed, and in the western rural areas an Interparish Catholic Rural Youth Club was started in 1946. Also, a Catholic youth center was opened in Kansas City, Kansas. Summer camps opened all over the diocese.

A view from the pulpit - Church of the Ascension in Overland Park

provided services for unwed mothers, placed orphans, helped resettle refugees, and arranged adoptions. Father William Finnerty was named director of Catholic Charities in 1964 and immediately expanded the agency's scope of service. Programs for disabled, elderly, imprisoned, undereducated, and sick persons were started under Father Finnerty, as well as counseling services and programs for inner-city children.

For 31 years, Father Finnerty headed Catholic Charities, stepping down in 1995. At the time of Father Finnerty's resignation, Msgr. Lawrence Corcoran, who was executive director of the National Conference of Catholic Charities, called the archdiocesan branch of Catholic Charities one of the best in the nation.

CATHOLIC CHARITIES

In 1945, the first archdiocesan branch of Catholic Charities opened with Msgr. John Horvat as director. Although Catholic Charities had no office of its own (it was located in the St. John the Baptist Parish rectory in Kansas City, Kansas) it made an immediate impact. Catholic Charities

Parishioners of the Cathedral of St. Peter gather for adoration in the parish chapel.

A beautiful summer day - Christ the King Church in Kansas City, Kansas

After the see was transferred from Leavenworth to Kansas City, Kansas, St. Peter Church became the new cathedral.

BISHOP GEORGE DONNELLY

During the summer of 1946, Bishop Schulte received word of his transfer to the Archdiocese of Indianapolis. Taking his place was the Auxiliary Bishop of St. Louis, George Donnelly, who was installed January 9, 1947. Soon after Bishop Donnelly's arrival, the see

Bishop George Donnelly

city of the diocese was transferred from Leavenworth to Kansas City, Kansas. St. Peter Church was designated the new cathedral of the Diocese of Kansas City in Kansas. Both in general population and in number of Catholics, Kansas City, Kansas, had far outgrown Leavenworth.

Bishop Donnelly followed the path of his predecessor, stressing the importance of Catholic education. Recognizing the need for Catholic higher education, Bishop Donnelly established a junior college in the former Catholic High School building next to the bishop's residence. The Benedictine Sisters formed the nucleus of the faculty as Donnelly College opened its doors in 1949 to the community to provide low-cost higher education.

Bishop Donnelly established Donnelly College in 1949.

The first cathedral in Kansas was this simple log cabin. It was Bishop Miege's first church

The old Cathedral of the Immaculate Conception in Leavenworth

CATHEDRALS WORLDWIDE are known for their elegance and beauty. Many are architectural masterpieces that can be defined as works of art as well as places of worship. But what makes a cathedral? A cathedral is not limited by size, architecture or decoration.

Without undergoing any physical change, any church can become a cathedral.

The cathedral is simply the bishop's church. It is where he presides over the liturgy, and symbolically, over the entire diocese. The name comes from the Latin word *cathedra,* which means chair. In ancient times the chair was a symbol of the bishop's teaching authority. Even today, a *cathedra* is an essential aspect of a cathedral. The cathedral is located in the diocese, usually in the see city in which the bishop exercises his authority.

Furthermore, it is the people's church. No matter what local parish Catholics may attend, the cathedral is their shared church, belonging to everyone in the diocese.

Bishop John Baptist Miege first established a cathedral among the Potawatomi in St. Marys. That cathedral was a simple log cabin.

When the Kansas territory was opened up to white settlement, Bishop Miege moved to Leavenworth and established the Cathedral of the Immaculate Conception in 1855. In 1864, Bishop Miege began construction on a grand cathedral that he had long desired. His cathedral was a true jewel of Leavenworth built

The interior of the old Cathedral of the Immaculate Conception in Leavenworth

Archbishop Keleher's *cathedra*, a symbol of his teaching authority

in Romanesque style. Upon its completion, the Leavenworth *Times* called it "the finest cathedral west of St. Louis." As Kansas grew, and Kansas City, Kansas, surpassed Leavenworth in population and size, the see was transferred to Kansas City, Kansas, in 1947, and St. Peter Church,

A statue of St. Peter with the keys to the kingdom inside the Cathedral of St. Peter

This stained-glass window in the cathedral depicts John the Baptist baptizing Jesus in the Jordan River

Next pages:
The interior of the Cathedral of St. Peter

which had been established in 1907, became the new cathedral.

Located in the heart of Kansas City, Kansas, the Cathedral of St. Peter is built in the Gothic style. The nave is lighted by six stained-glass windows on each side. Arches emerge from the five columns that align the church to form a vaulted ceiling.

In the liturgies of the cathedral church, the bishop exercises his pastoral role to teach, govern, and sanctify the diocese for which he is the chief shepherd.

The Cathedral of St. Peter constructed in Gothic style

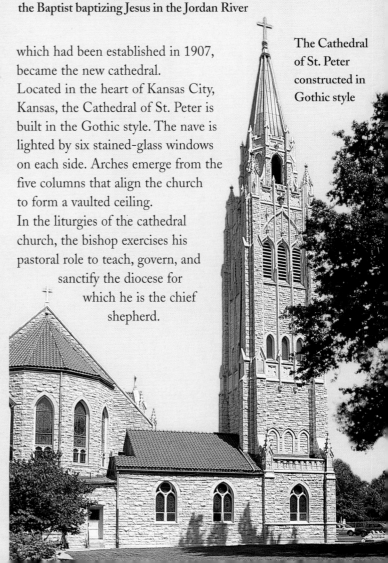

ARCHBISHOP
EDWARD HUNKELER

A flood devastated Kansas in 1951.

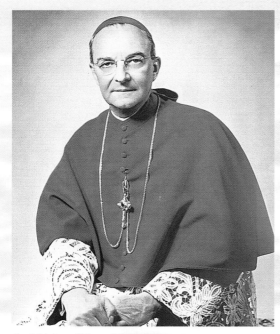

Archbishop Edward Hunkeler

Following the death of Bishop Donnelly on December 13, 1950, a native Kansan, Bishop Edward Hunkeler, was named bishop. Bishop Hunkeler had been bishop of Grand Island, Nebraska.

The marker on St. John the Evangelist Church in Kansas City, Kansas, shows the high-water mark.

Archbishop Hunkeler distributes Communion.

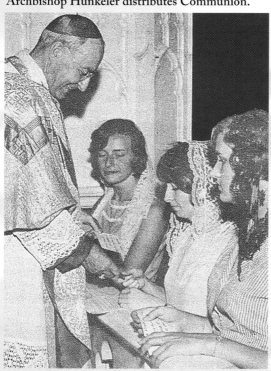

Upon his return to Kansas in 1951, things began to happen quickly. The two other dioceses in Kansas were restructured to allow the formation of the Dodge City Diocese. That same year a massive flood hit Kansas causing millions of dollars' worth of damage and destroying some towns. Several churches were severely damaged — some destroyed, never to revive. The bishop quickly organized a flood emergency committee to aid families devastated by the flood.

In 1952, Kansas was made an ecclesiastical province with Kansas City, Kansas, as an archdiocese and Bishop Hunkeler as an archbishop. Up until then the dioceses in Kansas were suffragan sees of St. Louis. On December 11, 1952, before a congregation in the Cathedral of St. Peter, the ecclesiastical province of the Archdiocese of Kansas City in Kansas was officially proclaimed.

Following years of stagnation due to the Great Depression and World War II, the archdiocese began to experience rapid growth. Many church facilities, built around the turn of the century, were in need of renovation or expansion. Also, the need for schools intensified as children born during the baby boom were coming of age.

VATICAN COUNCIL II

In 1958, Pope Pius XII died and Cardinal Angelo Roncalli was elected pope, taking the name John XXIII. Pope John convened the Second Vatican Council in 1962, undoubtedly the most momentous Catholic event in the 20th century.

Archbishop Hunkeler attended all four sessions of Vatican II. The emphasis was on the concept of the "people of God" in the modern world. The roles of priests, religious and the laity were redefined in terms of shared responsibility.

Father Thomas Tank, vicar general for the archdiocese, who was just a seminarian at

Pope John XIII convened the Second Vatican Council in 1962.

Vatican Council II

the time, remembers Vatican II as an exciting time for the church. "We were very much challenged by the renewal that was being undertaken and outlined for the church," he said.

It fell upon Archbishop Hunkeler to implement the changes of Vatican II throughout the archdiocese. The most visible impact of the council was in worship. The liturgy would now be celebrated in the language of the people; there would be a greater emphasis on Scripture in the Eucharist and the Sacraments; and the laity would have a more active involvement in the celebration of the liturgy. The all-English Mass became effective in October 1967.

45

Father Tank feels that while Vatican II was a tremendous moment for the church, one that strengthened the church, the way the changes were implemented could have been better. "Unfortunately, we tended to make changes and then educate the people afterwards. That wasn't a good process," he said.

FOREIGN MISSIONS

In 1959, Pope John XXIII wrote an encyclical that would have tremendous repercussions worldwide — *"Princeps Pastorum"* (called "On the Missions"). In that encyclical, the pope called on the religious communities of the world to partake in missionary activities in Third-World countries.

The call was answered world-wide, and the Archdiocese of Kansas City in Kansas was no exception.

A contingent of Benedictine monks from Atchison arrived in Mineiros, Brazil, in 1961. In the 30 years since, the monks have helped Mineiros grow from a small, undeveloped rural community to a thriving agricultural center. Early on, the monks introduced rice farming and worked with corn and cotton. They were also instrumental in breeding dairy cattle. Over the years, the Benedictines' focus has shifted from farming to education and pastoral and social efforts. The Benedictines' efforts have had such an impact that two monks originally from Atchison, Matthias Schmidt and Herbert Hermes, were named bishops in Brazil. The Benedictine Sisters of Atchison began their mission activity in Brazil in 1964. The Sisters have worked closely with the monks over the years, cooperating in pastoral and educational matters. The Sisters have been highly active in social work with the poor. The missionary efforts of the Sisters of Charity of Leavenworth have been concentrated in Peru. Arriving in 1963, the Sisters have had a tremendous impact working in the areas of women's rights, health and sanitation, and religious education. In 1981, the Sisters began a house of formation aimed at encouraging vocations from the native Peruvians.

In 1967, the Ursuline Sisters of Paola sent two nuns, Sister Roberta Allen and Sister Elizabeth Ann Nick, to Guatemala to work in conjunction

Benedictine Father Duane Roy visits with a family in one of the poorest regions of Mineiros, Brazil.

Two little boys of Talara, Peru, take part in a First Communion preparation class taught by the Sisters of Charity of Leavenworth.

with a team of missionaries from the Oklahoma City-Tulsa Diocese. Sister Roberta focused her attention on developing young people's artistic potential, but she was recalled after one year. Sister Elizabeth, however, was instrumental in starting a radio station that broadcast educational lessons to "radio schools." These radio schools — located in people's homes where small groups would gather for each day — would broadcast lessons on literacy, mathematics and health. In three years' time more than 24 schools were started with an average of 15 people in attendance.

The archdiocese has also sent a priest to South America. Father Marc Tillia went to the Diocese of Juarzerio, Bahia in Brazil in 1969 and has been there ever since. Father Tillia's "parish" covers an area about the size of the Archdiocese of Kansas City in Kansas and contains more than 100 villages and 40,000 people. Early in his career as a missionary, Father Tillia flew a plane to the remote areas he was responsible for, but since the early 90s he has given up flying because of better roads and danger from drug dealers shooting at his plane.

Today, through the Society of the Propagation of the Faith, some 30 missionary projects are supported in Asia, Africa and Latin America.

The archdiocese has also sent a number of lay volunteers to various foreign missions under a papal volunteer program called Pavla.

SAVIOR OF THE WORLD

While the Second Vatican Council was proceeding, Archbishop Hunkeler took steps to fulfill a dream — establishing a seminary in the archdiocese. In 1962, he launched a capital campaign to raise funds for a minor seminary. The campaign was a huge success, and in 1965 Savior of the World Seminary was opened in western Wyandotte County. It was Archbishop Hunkeler's hope that the seminary would encourage more young men of northeast Kansas to consider the priesthood.

The seminary opened with 66 freshmen and 31 sophomores. For 22 years, Savior of the World Seminary served the archdiocese well, offering high school seminary education to more than 600 young men. Close to 300 boys graduated from the seminary.

Savior of the World fell victim to the times. Throughout the 70s and into the 80s vocations steadily declined. Savior of the World closed in 1987. At the time, Archbishop Ignatius Strecker, who succeeded Archbishop Hunkeler in 1969, said, "This has been a most difficult decision. Yet in a sense, the decision was made for us by a declining enrollment, the shortage of priests to serve on the faculty, and the ever increasing cost to maintain the seminary."

Savior of the World Seminary opened in 1965 and served the archdiocese for 22 years.

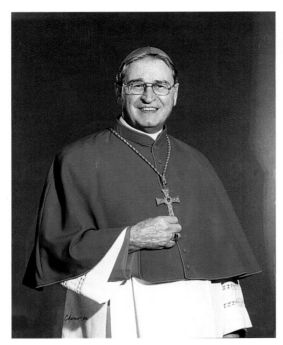

Archbishop Ignatius J. Strecker

Archbishop Strecker takes part in an ecumenical service.

ARCHBISHOP
IGNATIUS J. STRECKER

After 50 years as a priest and 18 years in the archdiocese, Archbishop Hunkeler retired in 1969 because of health reasons. He died the following year.

Succeeding him was another native Kansan, Ignatius J. Strecker. Like Archbishop Hunkeler, Archbishop Strecker had attended all four sessions of Vatican II while bishop of the Diocese of Springfield-Cape Girardeau, Missouri. Archbishop Strecker's first months

in the archdiocese were a whirlwind as he visited every parish, mission and institution. The following year, Archbishop Strecker began to concentrate his efforts on the spiritual and educational growth of his people and the implementation of the Vatican II documents. He especially focused on the role of the Church in the modern world and on increasing the role of the laity in the Church. He brought lay people into shared responsibility for the administration of church matters by directing that every parish establish a parish council and finance committee. Under Archbishop Strecker, the archdiocese was one of the first dioceses in the country to have a lay chief financial officer and an independent audit of the financial affairs of the diocese.

Archbishop Strecker established a central commission, comprised of priests, sisters and laity, to evaluate the archdiocese and set a vision for the future based on the theology derived from Vatican II. This commission studied almost every facet of archdiocesan life, including liturgy, family life, religious life, priesthood, education, communication, ecumenism, special needs, and social justice. It led to an archdiocesan-wide study involving all people.

During Lent of 1973, the people of the archdiocese were urged to participate in "Call to Share — Prayer and Study." Small groups met in nearly every parish to discuss various conditions and needs of church life and to make recommendations for action.

Archbishop Strecker blesses the people after Mass.

A rural life office was established by Archbishop Strecker to respond to farming concerns.

The response was phenomenal as more than 25,000 participants contributed to the effort. The study found the majority of recommendations pertained to the parish. Thus the archbishop left it up to individual parishes to determine how to implement those recommendations. In areas of larger concern, Archbishop Strecker spurred the archdiocese to action. A rural life office was established to respond to the needs of the farm community which makes up much of the archdiocese. A family life office was established and began putting in place policies and programs to assist engaged couples, as well as programs designed to enrich the lives of those already married. A criminal justice ministry was developed to promote reforms within the prison system.

Special ministries for the hearing impaired and religious education for the disabled were initiated. As a result of the Supreme Court's 1973 decision in Roe vs. Wade, which legalized abortion, respect-life and human-development programs were implemented. A particular concern of Vatican II was social justice. The council reaffirmed the Church's responsibility to the poor and oppressed. The archdiocese took notice. Catholic Social Services, a division of Catholic Charities, expanded its programs, and emergency assistance centers began forming all over the archdiocese.

Archbishop Strecker expanded Donnelly College to serve the educational needs of the poor in the inner city.

Shantivanam, a house of prayer, was established in the archdiocese.

In order to fund many of these new ministries — as well as existing ministries — Archbishop Strecker initiated "Call to Share — Responding to Needs" in 1975. This fundraising effort, which has evolved into the Archbishop's Annual Appeal, has remained an annual event. It provides the archdiocese with much-needed funds to continue its many ministries and charitable works.

St. Lawrence Campus Center - the University of Kansas in Lawrence

Archbishop Strecker also approached Father Ed Hays about starting an archdiocesan house of prayer. Father Hays accepted the challenge and Shantivanam was born.

"He shared with me his feelings that at the heart of implementing the decrees of the Second Vatican Council was a renewal of people's hearts," Father Hays said. "He believed that we needed in this diocese a place to pray."

Archbishop Strecker guided the archdiocese through a period of urban sprawl which saw the suburban population explode. Seven new parishes were established during this time, including five in southern Johnson County, one in Topeka, and one in Lawrence.

Archbishop Strecker also showed a strong commitment to Catholic education. He expanded the two-year Donnelly College to better serve the educational needs of the poor and disadvantaged with its move in 1981 to the former Providence Hospital building in Kansas City, Kansas. In 1989,

he formed the Institute of Religious Studies to assist in adult formation and training of religious education instructors as well as Catholic school teachers and laity.

Campus ministry was another emphasis of Archbishop Strecker's. He was instrumental in enhancing the existing campus ministry programs at the University of Kansas and Emporia State University. He also supported the building of the St. Lawrence Campus Center at the University of Kansas and the Didde Center at Emporia State and assigned full-time chaplains to those ministries. The Haskell Indian Nations Catholic Campus Center in Lawrence and the Washburn Campus Center in Topeka were also started under Archbishop Strecker.

BISHOP MARION FORST

In 1976 Bishop Marion Forst became an auxiliary bishop for the archdiocese after resigning as bishop of the Dodge City Diocese earlier that year. He had served 16 years as bishop of Dodge City. Like Archbishop Strecker, Bishop Forst had also attended the Second Vatican Council.

In his "retirement," Bishop Forst was an important asset by assisting with confirmations and attending meetings and ceremonial activities. He also served as vice-chancellor for marriage dispensations from 1985 to 1998.

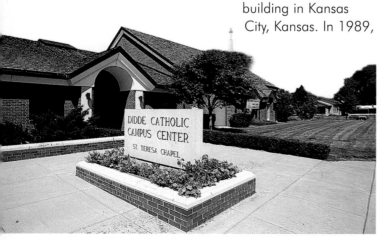

The Didde Catholic Campus Center - Emporia

Bishop Marion Forst

Upon hearing the news, Bishop Forst said, "This is fun for me. Rome has acknowledged that the Diocese of Leavenworth has been suppressed, and as such will never again become a diocese as it was. It retains, however, its glory in the sense of having its name restored as a titular see."

ARCHBISHOP JAMES P. KELEHER

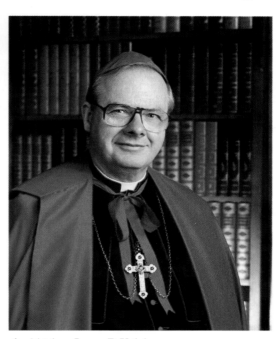

Archbishop James P. Keleher

Bishop Forst was definitely a man who loved people. In fact, in 1984 he ranked meeting the people throughout the archdiocese as one of the most impressive events in his life, behind attending Vatican II. "I have gone from parish to parish visiting people, joshing with a few, having a laugh with others, and always encouraging them to ask questions if they want information about the Church, the archdiocese or other Church-related issues," he said.

In 1995, Bishop Forst was named titular bishop of Leavenworth. Titular sees are see cities that cease to be active because of a merging of dioceses or the transfer of diocesan headquarters to another city.

As he approached the mandatory retirement age of 75, Archbishop Strecker submitted his resignation to Rome in 1992. A few months later the archdiocese had a new archbishop — James P. Keleher, formerly bishop of the Diocese of Belleville, Illinois. Archbishop Keleher's down-to-earth and folksy style endeared him to the people of the archdiocese almost immediately.

Bishop Forst talks with people following a Mass welcoming him to the archdiocese.

After an initial get-acquainted period, Archbishop Keleher began assessing the needs of the archdiocese in late 1994. Surveys were taken of priests, the laity and religious to determine the needs of the archdiocese. The archbishop also hired professional consultants to evaluate the archdiocesan offices.

The results of the survey led to the creation of new archdiocesan offices, including the family life office, stewardship and development, adult faith formation, and administrative services, as well as the expansion of several other offices to meet increasing demands. The archbishop also named two vicars general, Father Thomas Tank and Father Charles McGlinn, to help with much of the day-to-day administrative responsibility.

The archbishop also formed an administrative team to assist him in the leadership direction of the archdiocese. The team consisted of the vicars general, chancellor, executive director of Catholic Charities, chief financial officer, director of stewardship and development and the superintendent of archdiocesan schools. Archbishop Keleher has focused strongly on priestly vocations during his tenure, naming a full-time vocations director in 1994. Without the responsibilities of a parish, the director has been able to concentrate his efforts wholeheartedly on vocations

Archbishop James P. Keleher preaches to the people of the archdiocese.

to the priesthood. The approach has resulted in increased vocations being identified in the archdiocese.

In 1997, the archdiocese established the Catholic Foundation of Northeast Kansas, a not-for-profit entity designed to provide a means for people and organizations to support the charitable, educational and religious institutions in the archdiocese. The foundation provides estate-planning assistance, gift opportunities by which the Church or other related entities could be designated as beneficiaries, investment management services for parishes and schools, and distribution of earnings on endowed funds according to the wishes of the donors.

URBAN RENEWAL

While the 80s saw an exodus of people from Kansas City, Kansas, to the suburbs of Johnson County, the inner city struggled to survive. The Catholic Church, however, remained committed to the inner city.

The Gardner Plan was designed to ensure the continued existence of inner-city and rural schools.

Father Dennis Schmitz, vocations director for the archdiocese, talks to a group of youth at a youth rally in Kelly. Archbishop Keleher has focused much of his efforts on youth and vocations.

Archbishop Strecker was a staunch supporter of Donnelly College in Kansas City, Kansas, and its mission to provide quality education to an impoverished area.

The archdiocese operated Providence-St. Margaret Medical Center in Kansas City, Kansas, for 15 years. Upon its transfer to the Sisters of Charity in 1991, Archbishop Strecker used proceeds from its sale to establish the Providence-St. Margaret Fund for the future needs of the Church in Wyandotte County.

Archbishop Keleher has also been committed to the inner city. In 1997, he announced a plan to ensure the continued existence of inner-city Catholic schools as well as struggling rural schools. The Gardner Plan called for collaboration with local businesses and foundations to help fund the schools. With an estimated $1.6 million annual cost, the Gardner Plan focused on teachers' salary enhancement, capital improvements, scholarships, establishing a resource center at Bishop Ward High School in Kansas City, Kansas, and operations. "Whenever students are bettered through the educational process, they better the entire community," Archbishop Keleher said in announcing the Gardner Plan. "I want all of

our schools to be a marvelous experience, a fine education, for our kids. I'm here to pledge support so that our schools can give our kids the best."

Members of St. Joseph-St. Benedict have been instrumental in making their neighborhood safer.

In 1998 Sanctuary of Hope, a retreat and prayer center, opened in Kansas City, Kansas. Although ecumenical in nature and not sponsored by the archdiocese, the Sanctuary of Hope was the vision of an archdiocesan priest, Father Dennis Wait. "If we can turn people's hearts to God, that's the key to the rest of their lives," Father Wait said shortly before Sanctuary of Hope opened.

Other efforts to improve the inner city come from the parishes themselves. Most Kansas City, Kansas, parishes are members of the Wyandotte County Interfaith Council, an ecumenical group that encourages cooperation and collaboration in grass-roots efforts and outreach to the community. St. Joseph-St. Benedict Parish in particular has been highly active in making its community safer and better. Many parishioners are members of the St. Joseph's Neighborhood Watchdogs group that patrols the St. Joseph-St. Benedict neighborhood and has been successful in fighting crime. St. Joseph-St. Benedict Parish also entered into an alliance in 1999 with the archdiocese and Catholic Housing of Wyandotte County. The alliance has resulted

in new homes being built in the neighborhood. "The church is part of the city, and we care about what is going on across the street," said Father Michael Hermes, pastor of St. Joseph-St. Benedict. "Here we are building beautiful new homes. People in our parish will become new homeowners. It raises the morale of the whole neighborhood."

LOOKING TO THE FUTURE

As the church looked to the new millennium, Archbishop Keleher established a millennium committee to help guide the archdiocese into the new century. Based largely on the recommendation of the millennium committee, the archdiocese adopted Renew 2000, a parish process aimed at renewing Catholics' commitment to their faith. Renew 2000 groups formed all over the archdiocese as people gathered in small groups for a faith-sharing experience. In this new millennium the church in the Archdiocese of Kansas City in Kansas is growing in leaps and bounds. New churches are being built and old ones expanded.

A Renew 2000 leadership-training group meets at Savior Pastoral Center.

Archbishop Keleher believes the challenge of the new millennium is passing on the Catholic faith to our children.

Every year, hundreds of people enter the Catholic Church through the Rite of Christian Initiation for Adults. The Catholic population continues to grow as does the faith of the people.

Archbishop Keleher hopes, in this time of tremendous growth, that the archdiocese will look to the past and recapture the evangelical spirit the faithful had when the vicariate was first established 150 years ago. "Pius IX asked Bishop Miege to go to the territory and serve the Native Americans,"

the archbishop said. "He and the early religious who came to help did wonders in sharing the faith with the people who lived here. My dream is that we will do the same with the people who live here now. RCIA, Renew 2000, and Bible study are just a few of the ways we are deepened in faith and inspired to share it with others. Very important also are the vital contacts we make within our families, encouraging them to come back home to the Church.

"Very special in my dreams is what we can do to involve our young people more deeply in the life of the Church. The challenge of the millennium, I believe, is to pass on our precious Catholic heritage to our youth. If we can do that, we have been faithful to

Stained-glass window of the Good Shepherd-Sacred Heart Church in Leavenworth

INTERVIEW WITH ARCHBISHOP JAMES P. KELEHER

Where would you like to take the archdiocese as we enter this new millennium?
Evangelization is a key concept. It has three components that are very important for our diocese of the future. One is the personal/spiritual union. I would love to see all of us come closer to the Lord. Through prayer and reflection we can deepen our faith and our awareness of God's presence in our life and in the world around us. That is key to the conversion of heart, soul and mind.
That's what the Gospel is all about.
Second is to build up our communities of faith. I would begin with the family, which is, as the Pope calls it, "the domestic church." I think family life is under a lot of stress today. And then I would like to build up our parish community and our archdiocesan community. In other words, to strengthen Catholic family life in our archdiocese across the spectrum. We also need to acknowledge the broader Church, especially in Central and South America. We need to come together as brothers and sisters with a vision of the broader church and our connection with the Holy Father in Rome. The reason community is so important is because the whole atmosphere in America today is one of individualism and isolation.
The third thing is to have some positive impact

on our whole culture in America, making ours a culture that is pro-life, loving and compassionate.

What do you think is the strength of the laity of the archdiocese?
This the third diocese that I have been intimately connected with. I think per capita we have a tremendously talented and generous laity. They are extraordinarily talented. And they have a willingness to use that talent and the resources at hand for the good of others.
I see it all over the archdiocese. I see them on the boards and committees that I deal with. In the old days I would hear pastors in other dioceses complain about pastoral councils and tensions within the parish. I never hear that here. All I hear are the positive things about how our laity are helping our priests achieve the goals and the mission of the parish.

Much has been made of the Internet and modern communications in recent years. What is your take on today's communication technology?
Modern communication is a fantastic resource for good if you aim it in that direction. If you don't it could be a negative force. It's all in how you direct it. I think we have to be conscious that people today are molded by the structure of the medium. In particular, imaging, quick motion and sound bytes are what affect people. We always have to be aware of how we can be captured by the media as well as how we might utilize it.
I'm concerned to think that teenagers will watch 30 hours of television in one week, yet only spend 30 or 40 hours a year receiving professional religious education.

The media is morally neutral. It's how we deal with it and utilize it that makes it either good or bad. I'm afraid that too much of it is put to negative use.

With the number of older priests we have in the archdiocese, many people are concerned about a priest shortage and parish closings. How would you address those concerns?

I have never closed a parish in my six and a half years here. I would only move to close a parish if it was not a viable faith community. The future is bright in terms of vocations, but I think in the short run we have to be careful in how we utilize priests' potential, because priests are being stretched. I am very optimistic about the future. Parents are critical to vocations, which is an area we need to concentrate on. If you don't have parental support, discerning a vocation can be difficult.

Since you've been in Kansas City, you have made vocations a priority. How are the archdiocese's vocational efforts going?

We've gone from three seminarians when I first came to more than 20 in the seminary this year. I would love to see 35 to 40 in the seminary.

We have more and larger Serra Clubs in the archdiocese than anywhere in the world, believe it or not. It's incredible. That to me is a barometer of the support of the people for vocations, the fact that the Serra Club has taken off like that.

Invitation is critical. We have tried to continually invite young people to think about priestly vocations as well as religious life. We haven't always been good at that. You have to keep reminding people that God still calls as he always calls and that they need to discern in their own hearts if a religious vocation is what God wants.

The soil is fertile in Kansas. We are a Church where the Eucharist is held in high regard. We're a Church that honors the Pope. We're a Church that loves Mary. We have the elements that I think foster vocations.

The young people of the archdiocese have made a tremendous showing in recent years at World Youth Days, the National Catholic Youth Conference, and other youth activities. What do you attribute this level of involvement to?

Young people are beginning to feel the call to do something beautiful for God. Our parish youth programs are giving them opportunities to get involved.

In 1993, when I first came here, I began to meet our kids before I was even installed. At World Youth Day in Denver I met many of our young people. 1993 was a turning point in getting youth together for the spirit of pilgrimage and moving ahead and doing something about the world in which they live.

One of our plans for the future is to set up a youth camp that would be big enough to accommodate many, many of our young people during the summer months.

The programs we have now are too quick and there isn't enough room. Summer camps can be profound experiences for kids. They come back with a deeper spirituality, an experience of Catholic community, and a sense of wanting to do something beautiful for God and for the Church.

You have often said that the youth of the archdiocese are not only the Church of the future, but the Church of the present. What is the role of the youth and young adults now, and how might their role change in the future?

One of the exciting things for middle-aged people and older adults is to see that the Catholic tradition is being passed on. I can see it when older folks meet seminarians and how it touches them to see young people wanting to dedicate their lives to the Church.

When I see thousands of young people enthusiastic about Jesus, about the faith, about the Church, and about the Eucharist, that does something wonderful for me. An enthusiastic and young Church enlivens and gives spirit to the older Church. It gives great hope.

What are some of the challenges you see for the archdiocese?

We are moving from being a small archdiocese to being a mid-sized archdiocese. There is a tremendous growth in the number of Catholics, many of whom are professional, highly educated, very skilled people, moving into the archdiocese. One of our immediate challenges is working with that increased growth. We just opened a new parish, St. Michael the Archangel in Leawood, and we're looking for more property for future development.

The second challenge is tapping into a powerful youth movement. If there is one priority that a diocese has to have, it is making sure we are passing on the tradition from one generation to the next. If that doesn't happen your church dies. The archdiocese has been traditionally strong in Catholic education, and I expect that to continue. In Chicago, it's been probably 35 years since they've built a new Catholic school. We do it all the time.

We also need stronger catechetical programs because we have to face the fact that many of our kids do not have the opportunity to go to Catholic schools. It's important that we pass on our faith to youth through CCD and other kinds of formational experiences.

Campus ministry is also essential. The University of Kansas and Kansas State University are two of the most prestigious universities in the United States, but they are not Catholic; they are not even Christian; they are very secular. That's why we invest heavily in campus ministry, to provide a service not only to our own kids but to other young people who are coming to us.

Another thing I would like to see when my years here are finished, is a greater sense of family in the whole archdiocese. Parish life is wonderful, but a parish has to look beyond itself just as a diocese has to look beyond itself.

August 11   CLARE, virgin

Common of virgins (page 800), or Common of holy men and women, for religious (page 808).

OPENING
PRAYER

God of mercy,
you inspired St. Clare with the love of poverty.
By the help of her prayers
may we follow Christ in poverty of spirit
and come to the joyful vision of your glory
in the kingdom of heaven.
We ask this through our Lord Jesus Christ, your Son,
who lives and reigns with you and the Holy Spirit,
one God, for ever and ever.

August 13   PONTIAN, pope and martyr, AND
                       HIPPOLYTUS, priest and martyr

Common of martyrs (page 777), or Common of pastors (page 796).

OPENING
PRAYER

Lord,
may the loyal suffering of your saints, Pontian and
Hippolytus,
fill us with your love
and make our hearts steadfast in faith.
Grant this through our Lord Jesus Christ, your Son,
who lives and reigns with you and the Holy Spirit,
one God, for ever and ever.

Come, you whom my Father blessed, says the Lord, I ask you,
you who fed and shelter of the least of my brothers, or sisters;
what you did for me.
(Mt 25:34, 40)

August 14   MAXIMILIAN MARY KOLBE, priest and martyr

Introductory Rites

OPENING
PRAYER

Gracious God,
you filled your priest and martyr,
St. Maximilian Kolbe,
with real love for his neighbor.
Through the prayer of this devoted servant of Mary Immaculate
grant that in our efforts to serve others for your glory
we may become like Christ your Son,
who loved his own in the world even to the end,
and now lives and reigns with you and the Holy Spirit,
one God, for ever and ever.

Lectionary: Reading I (Wis 3:1-6, 9); Responsorial Psalm (116:10-13,
12-13, 16-17, for 30), with the refrain: Precious in the eyes of the Lord is
the death of his faithful ones.
Gospel (Jn 15:12-16), no 778. [or vv. 580].

PRAYER OVER
THE GIFTS

Pray, brethren . . .
We offer these gifts to you, Lord God,
with the prayer that,
inspired by the example of St. Maximilian Kolbe,
we may learn to offer our very lives to you.
We ask this through Christ our Lord.

There is no greater love than this; to lay down one's life for one's
friends.
(Jn 15:13)

Communion Rite

PRAYER AFTER
COMMUNION

Let us pray.
Pause for silent prayer, if this has not preceded.
Lord Jesus,
renewed by your body and blood,
we pray that the same fire of charity
which St. Maximilian Kolbe drew from this eucharistic
banquet
may also inflame our hearts
with heroic love for others.
You live and reign for ever and ever.

2

THE PARISHES

The Catholic Church is people — the people of God. This worldwide family is a people of prayer, a people of faith and a people of life. Catholicism is lived in our hearts, homes, parishes, schools and workplaces. From the mid-1800s to the present, the life of the church has been lived in parishes. The Church in Kansas began more than 150 years ago. Just as Bishop John Baptist Miege's charge was to bring the Gospel to the people of the wilderness, ours is the task of bringing Christ to a technological, fast-moving world. Between Bishop Miege and the year 2000, the mission of the Church has been accomplished according to the needs of the times. It has involved the shared efforts of bishops, priests, religious and laity. By virtue of our being Catholics in the Archdiocese of Kansas City in Kansas, we share in the total Church.

Over the past 150 years, the archdiocese has evolved from a frontier Church to one with incredible diversity. Many urban and rural parishes are a testament to the strong family roots set down more than a century ago, while our suburban parishes

65

St. Patrick Church in Osage City shows the wear and tear of time.

speak volumes of how the archdiocese has grown and continues to grow.

Many of our ancestors migrated to Kansas in search of a better life. They worked the land in a constant struggle for survival— somewhat akin to the struggles many of our farmers face today. But through those struggles they survived and preserved their faith despite often being miles away from a church or religious center.

As Kansas grew, towns began forming. So did Catholic parishes. Many of the early Catholic churches in Kansas were crude buildings — often no more than four walls under a roof. But these churches were built by people eager to preserve and pass on their faith. Some of these early parishes were established by people of a common ethnicity, others were just Catholics working towards a common goal. The results of these early parish efforts can still be felt today. In Kansas City, Kansas, and many rural towns, ethnic flavor and deep roots still remain strong in some parishes.

Our past has, in a sense, determined our future. Our ancestors built what has become the Archdiocese of Kansas City in Kansas. Through their commitment to the faith we have churches for worship, schools for education, parishes for spiritual renewal, and organizations to serve the poor and neglected. We have inherited the responsibility of continuing what they have built and passing it on to future generations.

People gather for Mass at Our Lady of the Snows Church on the Potawatomi reservation.

Holy Family, Alma

Although Catholics were settling in and around Alma in 1854, it wasn't until 1874 that a Catholic Church, Holy Family, was built. The parish was cared for by Jesuit priests until Father Francis Hundhausen arrived in 1880 as the parish's first resident pastor. Within two years a school was built and Father Hundhausen served as its teacher until a lay teacher was hired. In February of 1899, the church caught fire and was destroyed. The parish immediately banded together, and by August of the same year a new church was built. Fire struck again in 1913, destroying the high altar and much of the interior. In 1998, Holy Family celebrated its 125th anniversary.

fallen into disrepair, was razed. At the end of June the cornerstone for the new school was placed, and on September 8 the new school building was opened. In 1970 three Atchison schools, including Sacred Heart, were consolidated into Atchison Catholic Elementary.

St. Benedict, Atchison

When Bishop Miege put out a call for religious to help in his fledgling vicariate, the Benedictine monks were among the first to answer the call. The monks originally settled in Doniphan and traveled to Atchison once a month. However, Atchison began to expand and the Benedictines established a monastery and college there in 1858. A church was constructed the following year. For the increasing population in Atchison, St. Benedict's pastor, Father Augustine Wirth, dreamed of building a grand basilica in town. The cornerstone was laid in 1866, but several missteps by Father Wirth delayed its completion until 1869. The church was far from the basilica Father Wirth had planned; in fact it was little more than four walls and a roof. During the prolonged construction of the church, the parish purchased a building for the parish school. In 1891 a tower was added to the east side of the church. A second tower was added in 1905.

Sacred Heart, Atchison

In the late 1870s, with a booming population in Atchison, the Catholics on the west side of town made a request to the pastor of St. Benedict Parish (which had long been established) for a more convenient place of worship. To accommodate those requests, Father Peter Kassens, OSB, bought four lots in west Atchison in 1882, for the purpose of building a church. In October of that year, the cornerstone for a building, which would serve as both a church and school, was laid. In 1893, a new brick church was built. Shortly after completion, a fire caused considerable damage to the roof. In May 1929 the old school building, which had

St. Joseph Parish, Atchison

As early as 1924, diocesan planners envisioned the need for a third parish in Atchison. Property for a school was purchased that year, and in 1927, St. Joseph School opened. But it wasn't until 1948 that establishment of St. Joseph Parish was authorized. The cornerstone was laid October 9, 1949, and the first Mass was celebrated on Christmas Eve of that year. When the three Atchison schools were consolidated in 1970, the old St. Joseph School was torn down.

St. Patrick, Atchison

St. Patrick Parish, located eight miles south of Atchison, was started in 1857 by Benedictine Father Augustine Wirth. On his first visit, Father Wirth walked 18 miles from Doniphan. After his first Mass his parishioners presented him with a horse. Father Wirth continued to visit the parish once a month on horseback. In the fall of 1859, land was given to the parish and Father Wirth promptly built a small church. In June 1860, the church was destroyed in a storm. A new church was built a year later. In 1866, yet another new church was built. That church still stands today, making it the oldest Catholic church in continuous use in Kansas. When the new church was completed, the old church served as a school, which closed in 1966.

St. Michael, Axtell

St. Michael Parish began in 1881 as an offshoot of the now-closed St. Bridget Parish near Axtell. The first church was built in 1883 with Father J.M. Burk as its first pastor. The first church was physically moved to a new site in 1890. A school was started in 1891 but closed three years later because so few students were enrolled. At the turn of the

century, with an increasing population in Axtell, and the old church falling into disrepair, Father Burk made plans for a new church. The foundation was laid in 1903, and the church was completed in 1906. In 1913, after years of prodding by the pastor, the parish agreed to once again start a school. The school's basement was built that year, but a total crop failure in the area hampered the school's progress. It was finally completed in 1917 and was staffed by Benedictine Sisters. In the 1950s, the school was torn down and replaced by a new building.

Sacred Heart, Baileyville

In 1911, a group of Catholics in Baileyville discussed starting a parish there. A petition was circulated and presented to Bishop Thomas Lillis. The bishop approved the idea and on March 10, 1912, Sacred Heart Parish's first Mass was said. A

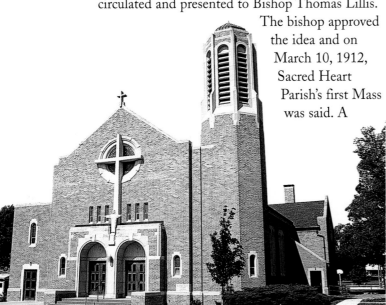

combination church and school was also built that year. In 1924, the parish made plans for a new church. This new building had a "temporary" roof put on it in 1925 with the hopes of completing the entire structure within five years. That never came to be as the Great Depression struck, causing the upper portion of the church to be postponed. In 1952, the cornerstone of a new church was placed, and on January 27, 1954, Archbishop Edward Hunkeler celebrated the first Mass in the new Gothic-style church. The people of Sacred Heart have strong German roots and most are farmers or retired farmers. The parish is very much devoted to the pro-life cause, having erected a memorial for aborted babies in the parish cemetery and a sign along the main highway.

Annunciation, Baldwin

In 1857, a Jesuit priest, Father Paul Ponziglione, established a missionary station near Baldwin. Father Ponziglione came from the Osage mission near what is now St. Paul, to celebrate Mass. In 1859 a small stone church was built and named Annunciation of the Blessed Virgin Mary. By 1893, the stone church had become too small for the growing congregation, and plans were made to build a new one. The new church was soon completed. In 1907 an addition was made to the church, consisting of two rooms to be used by the pastor while staying in Baldwin. At the same time, new windows and a new altar were added to the church. Urban sprawl hit Baldwin in the 1980s and Annunciation began to grow. In 1989, the parish broke ground for a new church, which was completed and dedicated the following year.

Holy Angels, Basehor

The first Holy Angels Church was built in 1866 in the community known as Hoge. Father Aloysius Laigneil, SJ, was the first pastor. Before then, Catholics around Hoge and Basehor were cared for by priests stationed in Leavenworth. In 1924, the parish moved to Basehor to build its third church. The parish was mainly a community of farmers until the 1970s when people started to leave the city for the suburbs and small towns. In 1974 there were 80 families at Holy Angels. Today there are 485. There are a few farm families left, but the majority of parishioners commute to jobs in the city. Holy Angels has demonstrated a generous spirit over the years. In 1982, they answered the call to feed the hungry at St. Mary's Food Kitchen and continue to send food and workers there each month. The parish also adopts several families each Christmas, ensuring that each family member has gifts. In 1998 two truck-loads of gifts were collected. Parishioners also collect canned goods for the Leavenworth Assistance Center.

St. Malachy, Beattie

St. Malachy Parish was established in 1879 as a direct result of an increasing Catholic population in Marshall County. Construction of the first church began in 1880 and was completed in 1882. A large German population settled near Beattie in the late 1800s resulting in Mass being said in German and English on alternating Sundays.

For years in the early 1900s several pastors tried to convince the St. Malachy parishioners to build a new church. Each time they were met with resistance. Finally, in 1921, a young priest, Father William Nelligan, was named pastor of St. Malachy and convinced the people to build a new church. It was completed in 1924. In 1929, the parish opened a school staffed by Benedictine Sisters. The school operated until 1969, when it became the victim of declining students and dwindling religious vocations to staff it. In 1971, the church underwent an extensive remodeling.

St. Benedict, Bendena

St. Benedict Parish can trace its roots back to 1855 when Benedictine Father Henry Lemke went once a month to celebrate Mass. Several priests cared for the spiritual needs of the Catholics in Bendena until 1861 when the parish received its first resident pastor, Benedictine Father Thomas Bartl. Father Bartl turned his attention toward the building of a church, helping do much of the work himself. In 1865, the church was finished. Some 30 years later, the parish outgrew the church and a new one was built. On May 25, 1903, a tornado swept through Bendena destroying the church, but not for long. Parishioners banded together, and by December of the same year a new church had been built with little debt, a church that still stands today.

St. Columbkille, Blaine

The early settlers of Blaine were Irish immigrants who were living in poverty in St. Louis. Seeing the plight of these immigrants, Father T. Ambrose Butler, a priest of the Diocese of Leavenworth, and himself an Irish immigrant, organized the Irish and convinced them that they could find a home on the plains of Kansas. Those immigrants arrived in Frankfort and made their way about 15 miles south, naming their settlement Butler City after Father Butler. Later, because there was already

a Butler City in Kansas, the settlement was renamed Blaine. Father Bernard Hudson arrived at the settlement in 1880 as the first resident priest. The first church was built the following year. In 1908 a new church was built and the old sold at an auction. In 1919, the parish opened a school staffed by Benedictine Sisters. The school was destroyed in 1927 by a fire that almost took the church with it as well. A new school was completed in 1928. The school eventually closed in 1966.

St. Elizabeth, Blue Rapids

St. Elizabeth Church was built in Irving in 1913 after the parishioners of St. Wenceslaus, eight miles southwest of Irving, voted against moving their church to Irving. Herman Fiegener, the parish's largest donor, asked that the parish be named after his mother, Elizabeth. The church, along with all the other buildings in Irving, needed to be moved to Blue Rapids in 1961 because Tuttle Creek Reservoir would be built over the area.

Sacred Heart, Bonner Springs

In the late 1800s, Catholic families began to settle around Bonner Springs. With no nearby church, the families traveled many miles over bad terrain to attend Mass. Father Michael Simmer, pastor of Holy Family Parish, Eudora, who attended to the spiritual needs in the area, proposed building a church in Bonner Springs. At the same time the Christian Church in town was preparing to build a new church and offered its old church to the Catholics for $700. The sale was approved, and on August 8, 1900, the building was dedicated. As the population of Bonner Springs continued to rise, so

St. Patrick, Corning

Before any parish was established in Corning, Catholics had to travel 25 miles to get to Mass. Apparently deciding enough was enough, the Catholics of the area decided to build a church of their own near Soldier. The simple church was completed in 1892 and cared for by priests in the area. In the late 1920s, as the population began to shift, the parish relocated to Corning. A new church and school were finished in 1929. In 1956 a new church was built. It was blessed June 21, 1956, by Archbishop Edward Hunkeler.

did the need for a larger church. In 1921 a new brick church was completed. In 1955, Father Michael Moriarty became pastor and began promoting the idea of a parish school. Parishioners liked the idea and launched a fund drive. The new school was dedicated on September 14, 1958. A tragedy struck on June 30, 1996, when Sacred Heart Church was destroyed by arson. As a result of an evaluation of the parish's future needs, the parish boundaries were changed in 1998. A piece of land was purchased in Shawnee.

St. Francis Xavier, Burlington

In 1871, a small group of Catholics around Burlington organized into a parish. Although there were little more than 10 families at the time, they contributed money and labor towards a church. In June 1871, the cornerstone for the church was laid and Mass was said monthly by priests from Scipio, Humboldt and Emporia. In just a few short years, parish membership grew so large that the church needed an addition. The parish continued to grow, and the old church began to crumble. After the turn of the century a new church was built. The church was dedicated in 1902.

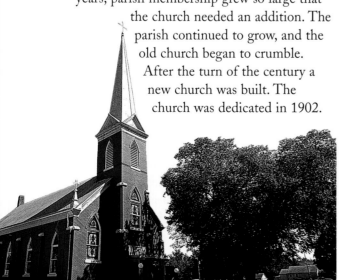

Sacred Heart, Delia

Sacred Heart Parish was established in 1908 when the old Holy Cross Parish that served both Emmett and Delia was broken up so that each town could have its own parish. Construction on a church began in 1908 and was completed the following year. That church still stands today. In 1993 the parish became a stational church and was administered by Immaculate Conception Parish, St. Marys. As a stational church, Sacred Heart has no resident pastor or regular Sunday Mass. Despite Sacred Heart's change in status, the parish community remains close and dedicated. In 1996, the church was given a facelift as several life-long parishioners raised money to paint and clean the church. Money was also raised to put a new roof on the church. In 1999 the parish had revival of sorts: CCD classes began once again, and Easter Mass was celebrated.

St. John, Doniphan

The first Mass in Doniphan was offered by Bishop John Miege in 1856. Later that year, Bishop Miege sent Benedictine Father Henry Lemke to Doniphan to establish a parish. Construction on the first church began in 1856. It was destroyed by fire in 1863. A new church was built in 1867. In 1891, an addition was built onto the church. A year later, stained-glass windows were added. In 1909, a large fresco was painted on the interior of the church, and in 1962, the interior was redecorated. In 1990, regular Masses ceased in Doniphan, as St. John was declared a stational church. In 1992, the church was leased to the Atchison County Historical Society for exhibit to the public.

St. Lawrence, Easton

St. Lawrence Parish was founded in 1878. The first Mass, offered by Father William Smith, was said in a railroad section house. Soon after that first Mass, Father Smith made plans to build a church. On horseback he visited the scattered families in the area seeking funds. Within a year a church was built. Over time, the parish began to

grow, and by 1916 a larger church was needed. Support for the new church was great and by the summer of 1916 the cornerstone was laid. The following spring, the Roman-style church was completed and dedicated.

Assumption, Edgerton

Assumption Parish dates back to 1857 when a few Catholic families settled in Johnson and Miami Counties. Father Bernard Donnelly offered Mass for the families from time to time. Although these families numbered under ten, they wanted a church, and Father Donnelly was happy to oblige. A log church was built and the first Mass was said in April, 1858. Just nine years later, a larger, stone church was built south of the log one. Thanks in part to the nearby railroad, the population around Edgerton grew, necessitating a new church, which was built in 1893.

St. Ann, Effingham

St. Ann Parish was established in 1867 and served by the Benedictine priests from St. Benedict's Abbey in Atchison. Father Placidus McKeever, the parish's first pastor, oversaw the construction of the first church, which began in June, 1872, and was completed in September, 1876. A school was started in a two-room building west of the church in 1907. A new four-room school building was constructed in 1928 and was used until the school was closed in 1969. The original ethnic makeup of St. Ann included people of Irish and German ancestry. Many of the current families are third- and fourth-generation farmers. Mass is offered daily; there is a weekly Novena to Our Lady of Perpetual Help. The Knights of Columbus and Altar Society are also active. With many generational families a part of the parish makeup, parishioners have formed a strong bond and know they can rely on each other in times of crisis or need.

St. Patrick, Emerald

In the 1850s Irish immigrants, seeking to escape a terrible famine in their homeland, settled in Anderson County and founded Emerald. The settlers' spiritual needs were cared for by a priest from nearby Scipio who encouraged them to build a church. Taking the priest's advice, they completed a log church in 1859. By 1895, Emerald was a prosperous community and began making plans for a grand church. A magnificent Roman-style church was dedicated

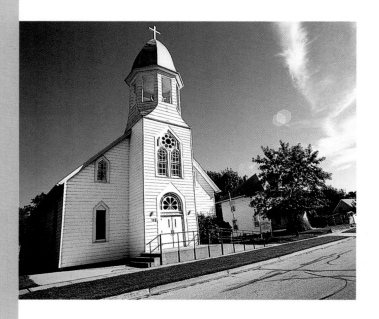

November 22, 1899, and became known as "The Cathedral of the Plains." In 1939, lightning struck the church and it burst into flames. Nothing was salvaged. A new church was built the following year, which still stands today. St. Patrick Parish is a farming community revolving around the church with weekend Masses, CCD classes, dinners and get-togethers. The small congregation grows steadily as more and more families move to the rural area and commute to work. St. Patrick Church is the focal point of its area as it sits atop a big hill where, on a clear day, there is a view for miles around.

Holy Cross, Emmett

Holy Cross Parish was established in 1881, four miles south of what is currently Emmett. It was cared for by Jesuit priests from nearby St. Marys. The basement for a church was completed in January 1882, and a temporary roof was built. Mass was said in the basement for seven years as work on the upper portion of the church slowly progressed. In 1908, the Union Pacific Railroad completed a line across the plains, and the towns of Emmett and Delia

were created. The parish was divided so that each town could have its own parish. In the division, the Delia parish received the main altar and Emmett received the church bell. All other items were divided equally. Construction of a church and school began in 1908 and was completed the following summer. The school, which was operated by the Sisters of Charity, opened in September 1907 and continued until 1968. Holy Cross has a strong group of parishioners dedicated to the continued existence of the parish.

Sacred Heart, Emporia

The first Mass in Emporia was celebrated by Jesuit Father Paul Ponziglione in the home of T.L. Ryan. Father Ponziglione made periodic visits to the Native Americans at the Osage Mission, and would often stop at the Ryan home to say Mass. In 1872, Father Joseph Perrier began making regular visits to Emporia, celebrating Mass in the courthouse. The first church was built in 1874. In 1880 the Franciscans were given charge of the growing Emporia parish. A new combination church and rectory was built in 1881, and a school in 1883. The turn of the century saw an increasing Hispanic population in Emporia. They were befriended by Father Berthold Stauback, pastor of Sacred Heart, and were a large part of the parish until they built their own church, St. Catherine, in 1923. In 1993, the Franciscans ended their more-than-100-year association with Sacred

Heart when they were called to serve closer to their province in Cincinnati. Sacred Heart has been a staunch supporter of Catholic education. The school serves students from pre-school through sixth grade. The annual Mexican supper, benefiting the school, has become a much-anticipated event in Emporia.

St. Catherine, Emporia

In the early 1900s, the Hispanic population in Emporia began to grow steadily. For a time the Hispanic Catholics in town attended Sacred Heart Church, but as their numbers continued to increase, they wanted a church of their own. That desire became a reality in 1923, when St. Catherine of Alexandria Church was built specifically for the Hispanics. The parish shared a priest with Sacred Heart. In 1993, St. Catherine, with under 50 families, was in danger of being closed. But thanks to an ambitious effort to reach more of Emporia's Hispanic population, the parish has not only survived but thrived in recent years.

St. John Vianney, Eskridge

Catholics were not always welcomed in Eskridge. In the 1920s the Ku Klux Klan sought to disenfranchise Catholics there. The first Catholic influence in Eskridge was simple street-preaching by priests from surrounding towns in the 1940s. Through this form of evangelization, a core group of Catholics was formed, and on October 17, 1943, the first Mass in Eskridge was celebrated in the American Legion Hall. But as Catholics sought to purchase an old stone church to convert for their own place of worship, longtime prejudices surfaced. The Christian Church, who owned the stone church, refused to sell their buildings to Catholics. An intermediary was necessary to secure the building, which was dedicated on June 25, 1944. Father Patrick Fitzgerald was named the first pastor.

Holy Family, Eudora

In 1859, the settlers around the Eudora area asked Bishop John Miege to send a priest. The request was granted. Father Lewis Guenther celebrated the first Mass in Eudora. For years, Mass was celebrated once a month in a store on Main Street. As the town's Catholic population grew, the store quickly became too small and an effort was made to build a church. A small sandstone church was completed in 1864. The church was used until 1963, when a new church and school were built. In 1981 a group launched a restoration effort for the old church, which had fallen into disrepair. Their efforts were successful and the old church is opened occasionally for viewing.

In the 1880s, the town's name was changed to Fidelity. In 1894 a new stone church was built. This church was destroyed by fire in May 1922, but many of the items inside were saved by parishioners. Construction on a new Gothic-style church began later that year. Although details are sketchy, there was a parish school in Fidelity as far back as 1886. That school closed in 1959.

St. Joseph, Flush

A Jesuit priest began making trips on horseback to Flush as far back as 1855, celebrating Mass in the homes of the scattered Catholics in the area. In 1868, a small stone church was built, and the first Mass was celebrated Christmas Day. In 1879,

St. Augustine, Fidelity

The early settlers around Fidelity were cared for by the Benedictine priests located in Atchison. In 1860, nine children from the area were baptized. In 1865, the community's first church was built. The town was named St. Augustine in honor of Father Augustine Wirth, one of the earliest circuit-riding priests to serve the area.

a school was built and staffed by a lay teacher. As the population began to grow at the turn of the century, a new church became necessary. This larger, Gothic structure was completed in 1901. In 1916, a new school building was constructed. In 1924, the interior of the church was redecorated. In 1935, Father Joseph Biehler was named pastor of St. Joseph and stayed until his death 61 years later. The parish school closed in 1976.

St. Ignatius, Ft. Leavenworth

A chapel exclusively for Catholic worship was built on the fort in 1871. The present structure was built in 1889 by the Diocese of Kansas City in Kansas. In July, 1967, the chapel's property title was transferred to the U.S. Army by Archbishop Edward Hunkeler. The St. Ignatius community has a unique status in the archdiocese by reason of its military affiliation. Turnover is extremely high, estimated at about 85 percent each year, making the establishment of a parish community difficult.

Annunciation, Frankfort

As the railroad began to take root across Kansas in the 1860s, the town of Frankfort formed along the line. Most of the earliest settlers were Irish, with some German families figuring into the mix. Benedictine Father William Fitzgerald offered the first Mass in 1879. He later organized the Catholic community into a parish. In 1880 the first church was built. That church lasted 20 years before an increasing population necessitated a new church. The second Annunciation church was

dedicated on Thanksgiving, 1900. In just five short years, the church went up in flames. On July 4, 1906, the third Annunciation church was dedicated. Two years later that church would also be consumed by fire. Despite their bad luck, the parishioners of Annunciation persevered and built yet another church, which was dedicated on February 22, 1909. This church didn't suffer the disastrous fortune of its predecessors and received an extensive renovation in 1976.

Sacred Heart, Gardner

Gardner was another town organized along the route of the railroad. The early families of the area banded together and sought to organize a parish. With the blessing of Bishop Louis Fink, a parish was created in 1875 and named St. Columba. A small church was built that same year. As the community grew it needed a larger church. This church was completed in 1912 and renamed Sacred Heart. This once-small-town church now boasts more than 400 families of diverse ancestry and age. Along with the newcomers that began to move into Gardner in the 70s and 80s are many families with roots three to four generations deep.

Throughout the year, parishioners gather for many

fundraisers and social events, including the big Octoberfest celebration, that strengthen the Catholic community. To accommodate Gardner's growing population, Sacred Heart is planning to build a new church that will seat more than 1,000 people.

Tyrol, Austria, were placed in the church. In 1945, the parish began construction on a school. Work was slow, and the school wasn't finished until 1947. Despite the struggles of being a small-town school, Holy Angels is still going strong after more than 50 years.

Holy Angels, Garnett

The Catholic community around Garnett got off to a rough start. Organized in 1870, the area Catholics immediately made plans to build a small stone church. But a cyclone swept though town and destroyed the unfinished church. Starting over from scratch, the community buckled down and began building another church, which was completed in 1871. Holy Angels was cared for by Carmelite priests from nearby Scipio. In 1915 the cornerstone of the present church was laid. The Romanesque-style church was dedicated June 29, 1916. In 1928, stained-glass windows, imported from

St. Louis, Good Intent

St. Louis Parish, located five miles west of Atchison, began in 1880 with the building of a church named in honor of Bishop Louis Fink. In 1897, it was destroyed by fire but quickly rebuilt. St. Louis Church once again burnt to the ground in 1977. The people of the parish rebuilt the church a year and a half later. A parishioner made the altar, stations of the cross and podium in the new church out of trees damaged by the fire. The youth of the parish are very active, sponsoring a supper each year and picking up trash along a four-mile stretch near the church. They also have a tradition of going caroling to older parishioners' homes in December. St. Louis Parish, with 70 families, has a strong sense of charity within the church and the community beyond. Volunteers operate the CCD program and clean the church. The Altar Society sponsors a family each Christmas. On the first Sunday in August, the parish comes together for its annual picnic, which often serves 700 to 800 people.

St. John the Baptist, Greeley

In 1880, Catholics in Greeley were granted permission to separate themselves from the congregation in Scipio and start their own parish. The 12 Catholic families in Greeley, mostly of German descent, began construction of a church in 1881. On June 25, 1882, the new church was dedicated. The parish was cared for by Scipio's Carmelite priests. In the late 1880s a parish school opened. By 1918 the small building that served as the school had grown too small and a new school was constructed. As

early as 1936 plans were being made for a new church. But it wasn't until 1942 that the cornerstone was laid. Because of building restrictions brought on by the outbreak of World War II, the Romanesque church wasn't finished until October 12, 1944. Today, despite the parish's small population, it still provides solid Catholic education through its parish school.

St. Mary, Hartford

St. Mary Parish in Hartford got its start when Francis Brogan, an Irish immigrant, moved to the area in 1875. A devout Catholic who had success starting Catholic communities in Iowa, Brogan sought to do the same in Hartford. Unfortunately there were too few Catholics in the area. Undeterred, Brogan wrote a letter to the *Boston Pilot* newspaper, outlining the opportunities that awaited Catholics who came to Hartford. The letter got results, and over the next few years more Catholic families moved into Hartford. The first church was built in 1877, but soon became too small. The cornerstone for a larger church, still in use today, was laid in 1890. The church was dedicated in 1893. Some of the traditions that have been followed over the years include a parish rosary before weekend Masses, May Crowning of the Blessed Mother, Lenten Stations of the Cross, and various parish socials.

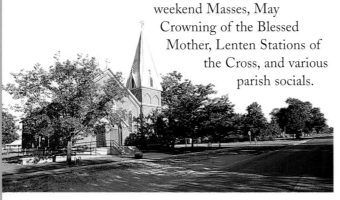

St. Ann, Hiawatha

St. Ann Parish dates back to the fall of 1882, when Benedictine Father John Stader was sent by his superior to investigate the need for a Catholic church. He found a few scattered Catholic families and began offering Mass for them occasionally. These families soon began to make inquiries about a church, at which point Father Stader began taking donations. The church was completed on December 21, 1883. Father Ferdinand Wolf, OSB, was the second pastor of St. Ann and quite an eccentric man. Father Peter Beckman, OSB, author of *Kansas Monks*,

wrote, "When Father Ferdinand prayed, he prayed loudly; when he moved, whether on the street or in church, he ran." One pastor complained, "It looks badly and endangers the limbs of the altar boys." Father Wolf was afraid of women and had little conversation with them, and he preached about the immorality of the hair style of the times—bangs. In the 1920s, St. Ann had a problem with the Ku Klux Klan, which had been actively campaigning against Catholics in Hiawatha, but no violence ever occurred. In 1957 the current St. Ann Church was built.

St. Dominic, Holton

A Catholic presence in Holton dates back to 1870, when Father Charles Coppens, a priest at the mission in St. Marys, came to the area twice a year—Christmas and Easter—to celebrate Mass. Thanks in large part to the railroad, more Catholic settlers began settling in and around Holton. By 1872 there were enough Catholics in the area to warrant a church. Although it was slow going, a church

was completed in early 1874. By 1891 the parish had grown so large that the church had to be expanded. As the town continued to grow, it became evident that a new church was needed. In 1922, the new Roman-style church was completed. In 1970, the parish's centennial year, the church interior was refurbished.

St. Leo, Horton

The first Mass in Horton was celebrated in a private home in 1887. By December of the following year, the cornerstone for a combination church and school was laid. The school opened in 1892 but lasted only three years. A new Gothic-style church was completed in 1916. Father Joseph Hildebrand became pastor of the parish in 1898, serving in that capacity for 25 years. Under his leadership the school was reopened in 1907 and staffed by the Benedictine Sisters. The school lasted until 1970, when it was closed for lack of teaching nuns. In 1979 the church underwent a major renovation.

Blessed Sacrament, Kansas City, Kansas

Blessed Sacrament Parish was founded in 1899 by Father Bernard S. Kelly, a young, newly ordained priest. Father Kelly's first order of business was to build a church. On Christmas Eve, 1900, Father Kelly said the first Mass in the new church. The top floor of the church was used to house a parish school, which opened in 1903. As the parish grew, plans were made in 1920 for a new church. The cornerstone for the new church was laid in September, 1924, and the first Mass was said Christmas Day, 1926. In 1950, the parish, now prospering, began construction of a new school. It wasn't long, six years to be exact, till the school needed an addition. The parish school closed in 1991. The building now houses the Blessed Sacrament Family Center, providing programs for disadvantaged children and families. In 1994, the church underwent a major renovation as an effort was made to restore the church to its original beauty.

Cathedral of St. Peter, Kansas City, Kansas

St. Peter Parish was founded in 1907. After a year in a temporary worship space, a church was built the following year and dedicated on September 7. The parish grew rapidly, necessitating a new church. A Gothic-style church was completed in 1927, complete with some spectacular stained-glass windows. With the transfer of the See city from Leavenworth to Kansas City, Kansas, in 1947, Bishop George Donnelly dedicated the recently redecorated church as the Cathedral for the diocese. In 1955, a new school building was constructed, replacing the half-century-old structure that had served as a school. At the beginning of 1998, the church underwent a major renovation of the interior. Later that year, the cathedral celebrated the 50th anniversary of its dedication. The people of the Cathedral of St. Peter have a strong sense of community and are a force for stability in Kansas City, Kansas.

Christ the King, Kansas City, Kansas

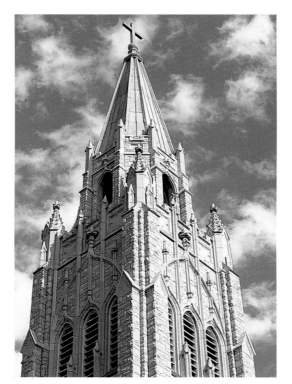

On April 19, 1939, it was announced that a new parish would be established west of Blessed Sacrament in Kansas City, Kansas. Construction on a combination church and school began later that year. On August 4, 1940, the building was blessed and dedicated. The parish school, staffed by the Benedictine Sisters of Atchison, opened on September 3, with 86 students. Christ the King is comprised of people from all corners of the globe. This melting-pot of ethnicity can be seen as music, food and customs of many nationalities are incorporated into parish programs, enhancing the beauty of the church and liturgical events. The parish is also driven by a strong sense of social justice and community service. Over the years, Christ the King has donated time, talent and money to AIDs education, the Duchesne Clinic, Crisis Pregnancy Clinic, Hurricane Andrew relief, Sanctuary of Hope, Bishop Ward High School and the Wyandotte Interfaith Sponsoring Council.

Holy Family, Kansas City, Kansas

In 1907 a group of Slovenian Catholics began to raise money for a church of their own. Bishop Thomas Lillis thought such an effort was impractical, but nonetheless, the Slovenians went ahead with their plans and secured a priest of their own nationality, Father Joseph Kompare. Upon his arrival, Father Kompare found that the church was not affiliated with the Diocese of Leavenworth. Father Kompare met with Bishop Lillis and attained the proper faculties to begin Holy Family, but the church was still not affiliated with the diocese. Two cottages were purchased, one for the rectory and one for the church. On August 15, 1908, the church was blessed and the first Mass celebrated. In 1910, the parish finally became affiliated with the Diocese of Leavenworth. In 1913, a school was built; it was enlarged six years later. In 1927 a new church was built. The church was refurbished in 1946. In 1959, the Holy Family School building was condemned and torn down the following year. On September 10, 1961, the new Holy Family School was dedicated. In 1989, the school merged with St. John School and became known as St. John/Holy Family School.

Holy Name, Kansas City, Kansas

In 1876, a small frame church capable of seating a dozen families was constructed. The little parish became a mission of St. Joseph Parish, Shawnee. As the area began to grow, a larger church was needed. It was completed in 1880. That same year a school was started, with classes held in the church. Although more than 40 students were enrolled in the school, it was closed after four months. In 1891, Franciscan Father Alexander Center became pastor of Holy Name and attempted to reopen the parish school, which lasted only two months. Another attempt to start a school was undertaken in 1901 in a new schoolhouse built by the parish. This one succeeded, and in 1902 the Benedictine Sisters of Atchison took over the school. A new church was built in 1912, and in 1914 the Ursuline Sisters of Paola took charge of the parish school. The parish boundaries were divided in 1923, with the residents of the southern half forming a new parish, St. Agnes in Roeland Park. A new Holy Name School was completed and dedicated in 1953. In 1986 the church was renovated, and in 1989 the stained-glass windows in the church were restored.

Our Lady and St. Rose, Kansas City, Kansas

Our Lady and St. Rose is the consolidation of two parishes, St. Rose of Lima and Our Lady of Perpetual Help. St. Rose of Lima Parish dates back to 1907, when it was carved out of territory from St. Mary Parish. The parish's first church was a two-story building known as "The Bakery." The ground floor was used as a parish school while the top floor served as the church. Our Lady of Perpetual Help has its origins in 1924, when Father Angelus Schaefer was appointed to organize an African American parish. The first Mass for that parish was celebrated Easter Sunday, 1924, in a vacant store. In 1968, changing population trends led to the consolidation of the two parishes into one community. The parish is known today for its hospitality, vibrant worship, and community advocacy.

Sacred Heart, Kansas City, Kansas

In the early 1900s, a number of people of Belgian heritage began to settle in the Argentine area and attended St. John the Evangelist Parish there. Soon, however, the Belgians began to desire a priest of their own nationality. They got their wish in Father William DeBoeck, a native of Belgium who was looking for such an opportunity. It was a perfect match, and on August 25, 1912, Sacred Heart Church was completed and soon became a

center for Belgian activity. In September of that same year, two Benedictine Sisters opened a parish school with 45 students. In 1954 a new church replaced the old one, which had long been inadequate.

Sts. Cyril and Methodius, Kansas City, Kansas

Sts. Cyril and Methodius Parish was founded in 1904 by Father Francis Simokik for Slovakian Catholics. For three years Mass for members of this new parish was offered in the basement of St. Mary Church until their own church was completed. A new combination church, school and Sisters' convent was dedicated in July, 1907. The school outgrew the two rooms it was relegated to in the 1920s. In 1922, a new school building was completed. The present church was built in 1938. In 1969 the parish school was consolidated with St. Benedict and St. Joseph schools to create All Saints School.

St. John the Baptist, Kansas City, Kansas

As the number of Croatians in Kansas City began to grow in the late 1800s, so did their desire to have a church of their own. At the suggestion of Bishop Louis Fink, the Croatians bought a piece of land in 1900 to house their future church, for which the bishop promptly donated $100. The cornerstone for this new church was laid May 15, 1900. At the same time, the Croatians sought to secure a priest from their homeland. Answering the call in 1901 was Father Anton Politeo. Father Politeo lasted only a few months. He left after displaying what has been described as less than exemplary behavior. The following year, Bishop Fink secured the services of another Croatian priest, Father Martin Krmpotic. In 1905, a parish school was started in the church basement. That lasted until 1907, when a school building was completed. The school aged quickly, and by 1929 a new school was built. Despite all the changes in the Kansas City area, St. John the Baptist still retains much of its Croatian flavor.

St. John the Evangelist, Kansas City, Kansas

In 1884, Bishop Louis Fink asked Father Thomas C. Moore, pastor of the now-closed St. Thomas Church in Armourdale, to establish a mission in Argentine for the Catholics attracted by work at the silver smelter plant. Father Moore quickly found that there were more Catholics than expected and suggested that the bishop find a resident priest for the area. Father Robert Loehrer arrived in 1886 as the first pastor of St. John the Evangelist, and immediately began the process of building a church, which was completed the following year. St. John the Evangelist is now consolidated with St. John the Divine Parish, which for years was the center for Hispanic spirituality in Kansas City, Kansas. St. John the Evangelist offers bi-lingual services and participates with other Christian churches in ecumenical services. Many of the long-time families have a strong commitment to Catholic education and support the parish's religious education program, Our Lady of Unity School, and Bishop Ward High School.

St. Joseph-St. Benedict, Kansas City, Kansas

St. Joseph-St. Benedict Parish is actually two parishes that came together in 1976. St. Joseph Parish was established in 1887 when 65 families, the majority of them of Polish descent, petitioned Bishop Louis Fink to start a church in the area in 1887. The following year

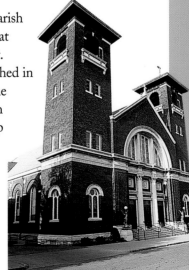

the first St. Joseph Church was completed. St. Benedict Parish was established in 1902. The parishes were consolidated in 1976 to form St. Joseph-St. Benedict Parish at the site of St. Joseph Church. In the 1990s, as many immigrants from Mexico arrived in the Kansas City area, a large Spanish-speaking community became part of the parish. These hard-working immigrants brought their customs of celebrating Our Lady of Guadalupe, a Palm Sunday procession, and fiestas. The Polish influence is also still very strong in the parish. The choir at Sunday's 9 a.m. Mass sings in Polish, and the annual Polski Day celebration in May is always a big event. St. Joseph-St. Benedict is also involved in promoting the well-being of its neighborhood. The parish works closely with several neighborhood organizations to improve the quality of life in the area.

St. Mary-St. Anthony, Kansas City, Kansas

St. Mary-St. Anthony Parish is a union of two of the oldest parishes in the Archdiocese of Kansas City in Kansas, dating back to the late 1850s. St. Mary was established in 1858 as the first Catholic Church in Kansas City, Kansas. The very next year St. Anthony was established by people of German heritage and cared for by Franciscan priests for 94 years. For more than a century, the two churches

existed as separate entities, each serving its own unique purposes. But as the population began to decrease and age, and with fewer and fewer priests available, the archdiocese deemed it necessary to merge the two parishes in 1980. The old St. Anthony Church was chosen as the home of the new St. Mary-St. Anthony Parish.

St. Patrick, Kansas City, Kansas

After growing weary of making the long trip to St. Mary or St. Thomas churches, a group of Irish and German settlers sought to build their own church. The dream became reality in 1873, when a white frame church was completed. That church lasted until 1954. Ground was broken for a parish school and a convent in 1947. The facility was dedicated in 1949. Since the parish had swelled to more than 500 families by 1954, Mass ceased being celebrated in the old church and commenced in the school basement for the next 13 years.

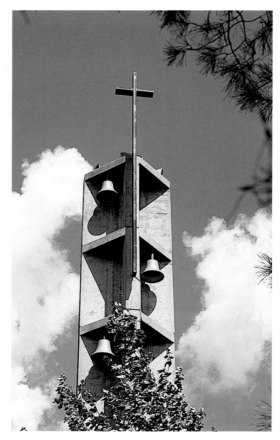

The cornerstone for a new church—the same one still used today—was laid in 1967. The parish has continued to grow, as evidenced by its more than 1,300 families.

St. Bede, Kelly

St. Bede Parish was organized in 1901 by Benedictine Father Charles Stoeckle, then pastor of Sts. Peter and Paul Parish in Seneca. The first Mass was offered on Passion Sunday, March 16, 1902, in a school building. On August 3, 1902, the first St. Bede Church was dedicated. In 1903, a parish school was started, offering Catholic education in Kelly until 1976. The Benedictine Sisters staffed the school during its existence. Like many other communities at the time, St. Bede grew rapidly around the turn of the century and the church was expanded. In 1913, the church was destroyed by fire. Two years later, the parish erected a new Gothic-style church.

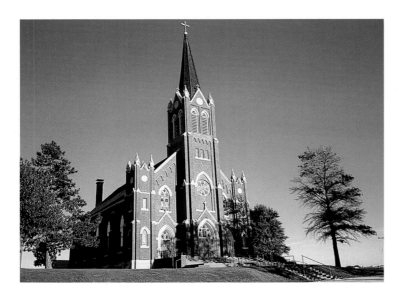

Sacred Heart, Kickapoo

In the spring of 1835, Father Charles Felix Van Quickenborne, SJ, visited various Native American tribes on the frontier of Missouri and Kansas. In July of that year he came upon the Kickapoo tribe, who had settled near Leavenworth. The chief of the Kickapoo attended a Mass Father Van Quickenborne celebrated and asked the priest to send a "blackrobe," as the priests were referred to, to reside among them. Father Van Quickenborne received permission and secured $1,000 in government money for the mission. Arriving June 1, 1836, Father Van Quickenborne began to build the first church in Kansas. In 1851, when Bishop John Miege was looking for a suitable place to build his cathedral, he was strongly divided between Kickapoo and Leavenworth but finally selected Leavenworth. In 1936, Sacred Heart celebrated its centennial, an event that was widely hailed in newspapers throughout Kansas.

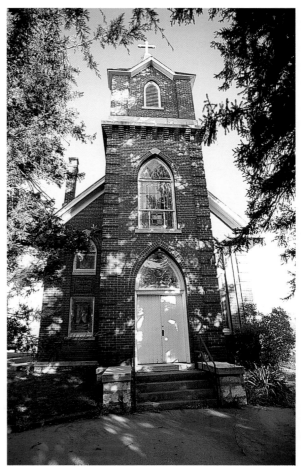

Our Lady of Lourdes, LaCygne

Our Lady of Lourdes Parish was founded in 1980 as a result of Father Patrick Fitzgerald's tireless work to further serve the Catholics of Linn County. After a piece of land was purchased for a church, Our Lady of Lourdes parishioners dug in and helped build the church with their own hands. The church was dedicated on November 28, 1982. Each autumn Our Lady of Lourdes holds a church bazaar that helps bring the parish together as well as reaching out to the community. Members of the parish also help out the local Meals on Wheels program each Thanksgiving. The parish was also a strong supporter in developing the St. Philippine Duchesne Shrine near Mound City.

St. Francis de Sales, Lansing

St. Francis de Sales Parish dates back to the 1850s, when a monthly Mass was celebrated by Jesuit priests in a small farm building in Delaware City. The Jesuits were the early initiators of missionary activity in Kansas. In

the 1860s, Delaware City rivaled Leavenworth in attracting settlers, but it eventually faded. As it became apparent that Delaware City would yield to Leavenworth, a movement was started to relocate the church to Lansing so that it would be closer to Leavenworth. Despite some strong opposition, the church was moved in 1884. In 1910, the church was enlarged and other improvements were made. In 1977, the parish broke ground for a new multi-purpose church building that would better serve its growing population. Construction was finished in 1979.

94

St. Francis, Lapeer

St. Francis Parish originated in the 1860s on the north side of Rock Creek, 20 miles southwest of Lawrence. In 1884, only three families remained on the north side of the creek, as the population shifted four miles south where present day Lapeer is located. The first church was torn down in 1884 and a new one built closer to the people. Mass was celebrated every fourth Sunday until 1925, when the parish was suddenly left without a priest. A priest from Osage City learned of Lapeer's misfortune in 1927 and offered Mass once a month until 1947. In the 1950s, St. Francis Church was remodeled to serve a growing population. The church was rededicated in 1954 by Bishop Edward Hunkeler.

Corpus Christi, Lawrence

Corpus Christi Parish was started in 1981 as the population in Lawrence became too much for the town's only parish, St. John the Evangelist. Father Frank Horvat was named the first pastor. The first parish church was completed in 1985. Ten years later, as the population in Lawrence exploded beyond expectations, the parish made plans to

build new facilities on a new site. Archbishop James P. Keleher blessed the new site on February 22, 1999. The first phase of construction was to be the building of a 1,000-seat church, a social hall, parish offices, and an education center. Construction was scheduled to be complete by September 2000.

St. John the Evangelist, Lawrence

In the autumn of 1857, Father J. J. Magee, a priest from Lecompton, celebrated the first Mass in Lawrence. In 1860, a small stone church was erected. It was dedicated September 30, 1860. On August 21, 1863, Bishop John Miege happened to be visiting the church when William Quantrill raided and destroyed much of Lawrence. The two men had a chance encounter, with the result that the church was spared destruction. Several parishioners were not so lucky. Fourteen Catholics were among the dead. In 1956, the present school was built and staffed by the Sisters of Charity. In 1986, Archbishop Ignatius Strecker asked the Capuchin order to take over the pastoral responsibility for the parish. St. John sponsors a wealth of activities such as its St. Patrick's Day party, All Saints Day bonfire, picnics in the park, annual fall dinner and the St. John School fish fry, to build fellowship and a feeling of community in the parish. Other activities seek to foster a relationship with the Lawrence community. The parish's annual Mexican Fiesta attracts more than 10,000 people every June, and Oktoberfest was voted the second best festival in the "1999 Best of Lawrence" poll.

Immaculate Conception, Leavenworth

On August 15, 1855, Bishop John Baptist Miege established the Cathedral of Immaculate Conception. The influx of settlers to the area following the Kansas-Nebraska Act of 1854 moved him to establish his church in Leavenworth, the first and fastest-growing city in the Kansas Territory. In 1864 he began construction on a magnificent cathedral, which was completed in 1868. This spectacular church served as the cathedral until 1947, when the See city was changed from Leavenworth to Kansas City. On December 30, 1961, the old cathedral was destroyed by fire. A new church was completed in 1964, with three of the bells from the old cathedral salvaged for the new bell tower. Consolidating the Catholic community of North Leavenworth began in 1954 with the closure of Holy Epiphany, the first African American Church west of St. Louis, and continued in 1970 when Kickapoo's Sacred Heart parish was transferred to Immaculate Conception. Immaculate Conception is still often referred to as "the Old Cathedral" and lovingly called the Irish church. There are still a number of local Irish families among its parishioners who go back many generations.

Sacred Heart, Leavenworth

As Leavenworth's population grew rapidly in the late 1800s, the need for a new Catholic church in southern Leavenworth arose. A small one-story school was started in the 1870s for the children in southern Leavenworth, and finally in 1885, Bishop Louis Fink established Sacred Heart Parish in that area and appointed Father Thomas Downey as its first pastor. The cornerstone for Sacred Heart's first church was laid October 17, 1886. That church lasted until 1926, when the cornerstone for the present Roman-style church was laid. All the Catholic schools in Leavenworth, including Sacred Heart, were consolidated in 1979 as Xavier Elementary. Sacred Heart Parish has always been made up of people of mixed ethnicity and ages. The parish also has a strong congregation willing to help the less fortunate through various community service efforts, as well as supporting the parish itself.

St. Casimir, Leavenworth

St. Casimir Parish began to take shape in 1888 when a small group of Polish immigrants from Westphalia, Germany, began to settle in Leavenworth. For a time the Poles affiliated themselves with St. Joseph Parish in Leavenworth, which had a large German congregation. In 1889, the Poles organized a society dedicated to St. Casimir. They also secured the services of Father Francis Kulisek that year as their advisor and chaplain. On Easter Sunday in 1893, the Poles were encouraged to start their own parish by Father Alexander Smietana, who had been assigned to the Society earlier that year. Within a year St. Casimir Church was completed and dedicated. The parish started a school in the church basement soon thereafter. The school was taught by lay people until the teaching Sisters of the Felician community of Chicago were secured. In 1979, St. Casimir School was consolidated with the other schools in Leavenworth to form Xavier Elementary. The present congregation includes people of many different nationalities, although the parish's Polish origins are remembered each year at a *golabki* dinner. *Golabki* is a dish native to Poland.

St. Joseph, Leavenworth

St. Joseph Parish was started in 1858 to serve the spiritual needs of the growing number of German Catholics in Leavenworth. The first church was dedicated on July 10, 1859. A school was founded later that year. On October 7, 1864, two Carmelite priests arrived in Leavenworth at the invitation of Bishop John Miege. They were immediately

transferred to St. Joseph Parish, beginning a long association between that parish and the Carmelites that still exists today. The German connection still remains strong despite the influx of other nationalities over the years. Even today German hymns will slip into midnight Mass on Christmas. The stained-glass windows that were brought over from Germany when the church was built are still in place and valued at more than $1 million. One feature that separates St. Joseph from the other parishes in Leavenworth is the many farm families that still belong, most of whom go as far back as five or six generations. One of the strengths of the parish is the large number of parishioners who are involved in ministry as lectors, Eucharistic ministers, ministers to the aged, and altar servers as well as those who donate their donate their time and skills to the upkeep of the church.

St. Joseph of the Valley, Leavenworth

St. Joseph of the Valley Parish, located nine miles west of Leavenworth, began in 1863, when a group of Catholics in the area were organized by Father Theodore Heimann. Father Heimann celebrated Mass for the group once a month in a private home. A church was built in 1868. That

same year an influx of Catholics filled the church to capacity. In 1871 an addition had to be built. By 1894, the little church was practically bursting at the seams and a new one was built and blessed by fall. The second church lasted until May 1, 1930, when it was destroyed by a tornado. By October the parish had built a new church, which stood only two years before being destroyed by fire on October 28, 1932. Despite the disaster, the parish persevered and built yet another church, which was dedicated in April, 1933. In 1986, the Leavenworth County Historical Society dedicated a historical marker outside the church.

Church of the Nativity, Leawood

The late 1980s were a time of astronomical growth in southern Leawood and southeast Overland Park. To accommodate the growing population in that area, Archbishop Ignatius Strecker established Church of the Nativity on June 28, 1986. Father Thomas Tank was named pastor of this new parish community that numbered 417. Groundbreaking for a church occurred April 8, 1990. The following year the parish started its own school. A spacious Byzantine-style church was completed in 1992. Being a relatively new

parish, Nativity does not have roots reaching back several generations, but it does have generous parishioners who are quick to give financially whenever the call goes out. The parish contributes more than $100,000 annually to several organizations in the greater Kansas City area and to Guatemalan Missions through its fifth-Sunday collections.

Curé of Ars, Leawood

Archbishop Edward Hunkeler established Curé of Ars Parish on June 23, 1959, in the flourishing area of southeast Johnson County. Until their church and school were completed in 1961, parishioners of Curé of Ars attended Mass in the basement of St. Ann Church in Prairie Village. By 1968, the parish had grown so much that a new wing was added to the school. As the population in southern Johnson County continued to increase, a new, larger church was needed. Ground was broken in 1978, and a new church that would seat 1,000 people was dedicated a year later. The old church was remodeled into a gymnasium. In 1984 the church was remodeled.

St. Michael the Archangel, Leawood

Citing an increasing population in south Leawood, the archdiocese established a new parish on July 16, 1999, with Father Bill Porter as pastor. The parish will be built on the northeast corner of 143rd and Nall in Leawood when the necessary funds are raised. In the meantime, Masses are being held in Prairie Star Middle School, located at 143rd and Mission Road. The first Masses were celebrated the weekend of August 14-15, 1999. Plans also call for a school to be built. Until that time, Church of the Nativity School will be shared by the two parishes.

Holy Trinity, Lenexa

Holy Trinity Parish started out as a mission of St. Joseph in Shawnee. In 1882 the Catholic community in Lenexa, at that time numbering about 20, decided to build its own church. The parish received its own pastor in 1906. By 1911 the parish had built a new stone church and renovated the old church into a school. The school opened in 1912, staffed by the Benedictine Sisters of Atchison. Soon the school became overcrowded and a new stone school was built. In 1975, the parish built a new church. That church was converted into a parish center when another church had to be built in 1996 to keep up with the growing population in Lenexa.

St. Joseph, Lillis

Catholicism in Lillis dates back to 1866, when the first Mass was celebrated in a log cabin in what was then known as the Cleveland township. Mass continued to be celebrated once a month in that log cabin until a church was built in 1872. As the railroad from Topeka to Marysville was being constructed in the early 1900s, a new town site was being laid out a mile from the church. Father William Michael, pastor of St. Joseph, was given the honor of choosing the town's name. He chose Lillis, presumably to honor his bishop, Thomas Lillis. As the old church began to fall into disrepair, the question of where to build a new church became a source of controversy. Many parishioners wanted to build the new church in Lillis, but eventually, it was decided to stay outside of the town. The foundation for the church was laid in 1912, but because of financial difficulties, the church was not completed until 1916. In 1953 and 1970 the church received major renovations.

Immaculate Conception, Louisburg

In 1886, the Catholic population in Louisburg had grown to the point where they felt a church of their own was warranted. Father John Redeker of Wea organized the parish, and by 1887 a white frame church was built. It proved to be a good church, lasting until a new one was built in 1954. Much of the work on the new church, dedicated November 5, 1954, was done by members of the parish. An addition to the church was built in 1985. The parish celebrated its centennial in 1987. That year also saw the church receive a major renovation.

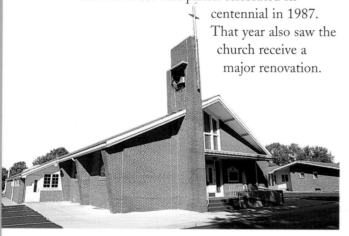

St. Gregory, Marysville

As far back as the 1860s Mass was sporadically being celebrated for the few Catholics in what is now Marysville. In 1877, a church was finally built as the Catholic population began to increase. The Catholic congregation quickly outgrew this church. In 1886, the cornerstone for a new church was laid, but because of a series of crop failures that took its toll on the

area, the church wasn't completed until 1894. Around this time a parish school was started. In 1903, the Benedictine Sisters took over the school. The parish's first school building was completed in 1906. As the railroad began to develop in Kansas, Marysville saw an influx of settlers. Talk soon turned to building a new church, but for financial reasons, the parish simply added on to the old church. In 1975, the 81-year-old church was finally replaced by a contemporary brick structure.

Our Lady of the Snows, Mayetta

In 1869, many of the Native American Potawatomi began leaving Kansas and headed to Oklahoma. Many of those who remained moved to the Potawatomi reservations near Mayetta. For years these Native Americans relied on irregular visits from surrounding priests to fulfill their sacramental needs in various locations. It wasn't until Father John A. Murphy arrived on the scene in 1911 that plans were made for a church. Rallying his parishioners to the cause, Father Murphy raised a substantial amount from them in one day and secured $1,000 in government money soon thereafter. Construction on the church began in 1912; it was completed the same year.

St. Francis Xavier, Mayetta

Mayetta is one of those towns that sprang up along the railroad. Missionary priests began celebrating Mass in the area as far back as 1886. Finally, in 1915, the Mayetta Catholics built their own Roman-style church. On November 11, 1958, the church was destroyed by fire. In 1960, after an extensive campaign to raise funds, a new church was completed. Archbishop Edward Hunkeler dedicated the church on June 26.

St. Aloysius, Meriden

The first Mass in the Meriden area was celebrated in 1879 by Father John Leary, who lived in nearby Newman. The following year Father F. X. Kraus came to Meriden. One of his first courses of action

was to build a church in town. In 1952 the parish was closed because Father Valerian Berger, OSB, felt the church had no future, since there were under ten families at the time. Eight months later, Father George Klasinski, who was assistant pastor of St. Joseph Parish in Topeka, reopened St. Aloysius as a mission of St. Joseph. The parish has since thrived, especially in the 60s and 70s. Several farm families, a commuter population from Topeka, and families who have chosen to build

in the nearby Lake Perry area form a natural and welcoming church community. St. Aloysius is active in efforts involving other denominations, and the parish has taken a leadership role for a local food pantry, God's Storehouse, which is staffed each Saturday by rotating congregations.

St. Pius X, Mission

In 1954, Archbishop Edward Hunkeler formed a new parish in Mission as suburban life became more and more popular. Father Francis Glowacki was named the first pastor. The parish broke ground for a parish building on February 27, 1955, and opened its doors for the first Mass on October 5 in a "temporary" space, until a "real" church could be completed. That never happened. The church continues to be used today. In 1996, the "temporary" church was renovated and redecorated. In 1956, St. Pius X School opened with nearly 300 children enrolled. An addition to the school was built in 1965.

Corpus Christi, Mooney Creek

Benedictine priests made regular trips to Mooney Creek as far back as 1857, caring for the spiritual needs of the few scattered Catholics, mostly of German descent. In 1872, the first church in Mooney Creek was built. An addition was built in 1887. That same year a parish school was started in the rectory but only lasted a few years. As the parish grew, so did parishioners' desire for a new church. The cornerstone for this new church was laid on June 12, 1907. In 1919, the parish once again started a school, staffed by Benedictine

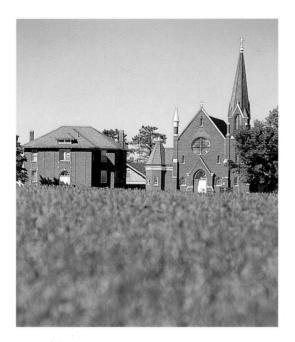

Sisters. This school lasted until 1966, when it was closed. Corpus Christi has approximately 60 families, many descendants of the founding families of the area. Over the years a deep sense of community has developed among the parishioners. Members are always ready to reach out to others in need.

Sacred Heart, Mound City

Following a street-preaching campaign, Bishop Paul Schulte collected funds during the Lenten season of 1941 to build a church in Mound City as a memorial to St. Philippine Duchesne, who had ministered to Native Americans at the Sugar Creek mission near Mound City. By 1942 the memorial church, named Sacred Heart, was built. It was the first Catholic Church in Linn County. Father Gerald O'Shea was named the first pastor. The parish currently has 65 families. Volunteers staff the CCD program, care for the altar linens and maintain the church and cemetery. As expected, the parish has a strong devotion to St. Philippine Duchesne.

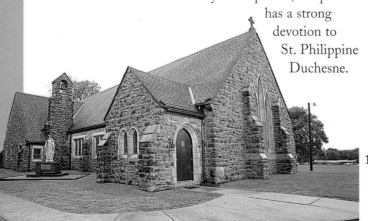

St. Joseph, Nortonville

There was much talk in the late 1880s of building a church in the Nortonville area. Before that time, the nearest place of worship was Corpus Christi Parish in Mooney Creek. In 1892, the cornerstone for a church was laid. The parish was cared for by priests from Mooney Creek. In 1904, Father C. J. Elast was appointed pastor of St. Joseph and began pushing the idea of a parish school, but to no avail. In 1905, Father W. J. Goldman became pastor and, like his predecessor, promoted a parish school. It took 10 years, but a parish school was finally started and staffed by Benedictine Sisters. Father A. J. Budreau became pastor in 1917 and began planning for a new church. But Father Budreau did not have the support of his parishioners, who claimed that his plans were too elaborate. Father Budreau was succeeded by Father Joseph Reich in 1929. Father Reich succeeded in getting a new church built in 1931. A new school was built in 1951. In 1982, the school underwent a major renovation. Catholic education continues to be offered in Nortonville.

Prince of Peace, Olathe

Prince of Peace Parish was established in 1979 to meet the growing spiritual needs in Olathe. Father Charles Andalikiewicz was its first pastor. On September 30, 1984, the parish broke ground on a new church-school facility.

104

than 200 parish children in grades K-8, while more than 400 children are enrolled in religious education classes. Because Olathe is the seat of county government, St. Paul, often joining with other area churches and agencies, serves the spiritual and material needs of less fortunate people such as the imprisoned and the homeless.

St. Joseph, Olpe

From 1883 to 1885 Franciscan Father Angelus Hafertepe took care of the spiritual needs of the scattered Catholics around Olpe. During those years, the desire to have a church of their own began to interest the Catholics in the area. In 1885, Olpe received a permanent pastor; a church was completed on August 6 of that same year. Today the parish boasts a school which provides solid Catholic education for the children of the parish. Since many of the founding families were German immigrants, St. Joseph Parish continues to be predominately comprised of families of German descent. The families maintain their German heritage by celebrating their culture through the preparation of certain foods, the language, and special traditions. One of the highlights is the singing of German Christmas Carols at Midnight Mass on Christmas Eve. Other special moments in parish life include First Saturday Marian Devotions, May Crowning of the Blessed Mother, Eucharistic Adoration, Divine Mercy Devotions, St. Anthony Devotions, Lenten Stations of the Cross and parish festivals.

The first Mass in the building was held Christmas Eve, 1986. As the population in Olathe continued to increase, the parish looked to build a larger church. In 1996, a contemporary church that can seat 1,200 was completed. Archbishop James P. Keleher dedicated the church on August 18, 1996.

St. Paul, Olathe

St. Paul Parish in Olathe is a community of more than 1,600 families united as brothers and sisters in worship through liturgy, in education through the teachings of the Catholic Church, and in service to all people in the name of Christ. The parish was founded in 1864 to serve immigrant pioneer families who settled on farms in central Johnson County. St. Paul is the home parish to deaf Catholics of the region because the Kansas School for the Deaf is within the parish boundaries. While a few families date back several generations, even to the pioneer farmers and railroad workers of the 19th Century, the demographic profile of the parish today is strongly suburban and somewhat transient. St. Paul School educates more

St. Vincent de Paul, Onaga

St. Vincent de Paul Parish began as a mission in 1881. It was founded by Jesuit priests from St. Marys. Later it was cared for by diocesan clergy from Blaine and other localities. Father Ambrose Butler from Blaine was one of the early pioneer priests to offer Mass and serve the community. Onaga had its beginnings as a railroad town. It remains an important link for trains delivering coal to several power plants. The present church was built under the direction of Father Edward Doherty. The cornerstone is dated 1948; the church was dedicated in 1950. The parish has grown considerably since that time when there were only a handful of families, usually numbering less than 20. Today there are 85 families. St. Vincent de Paul remained a mission until 1978, when Father James O'Grady became the first resident pastor.

St. Patrick, Osage City

The first hint of Catholicism in Osage City dates back to 1871, when a wedding was celebrated in town, perhaps the first Mass ever in Osage City. From that time on, priests would visit the area occasionally to offer Mass. In 1873, the first Catholic church was built in Osage City. Unfortunately, that church was destroyed by a cyclone the following year. It was quickly rebuilt. That church was also destroyed, this time by a fire in 1908. The cornerstone for yet another church was laid on April 17, 1910. The church was dedicated on June 14, 1911, by Bishop Thomas Ward. Following the Second Vatican Council in the 60s, the church underwent an extensive redecoration. The work was completed in 1971 in time for the parish centennial.

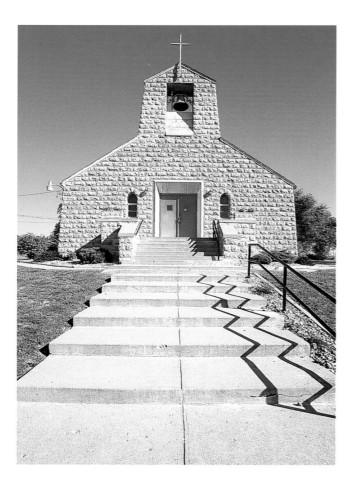

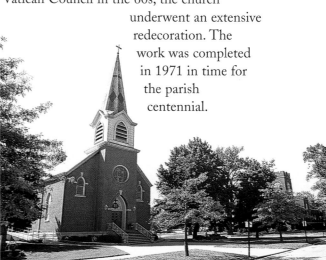

St. Philip Neri, Osawatomie

The history of St. Philip Neri Parish in Osawatomie is tied closely to the history of the city. Catholic missionaries working with the Native American Potawatomi were the first to bring the Catholic presence to the area. When the town was established in 1854, city planners—recognizing the importance of places of worship—included a church square, providing a lot for each denomination to use to build its own church. Only the Catholics and the Congregationalists chose to utilize those lots. Generational influence is evident in the parish life of St. Philip Neri. Several present members are descendants of those who helped found the first parish there and helped erect the first physical structure. Three subsequent churches have been built, each changing to fit the needs of an evolving congregation. St. Philip Neri School, 1921 to 1968, was the center of learning for the parish during its years of operation. Members of the parish are varied in age, but nearly homogeneous racially and ethnically. Mostly from Caucasian European stock, members of the congregation reflect the cultural background of Miami County. Liturgically strong, members have worked to keep the parish active through many changes—economic, political, and pastoral—during the 110 years of its existence.

Sacred Heart, Ottawa

In October, 1867, Father Paul Ponziglione arrived in Ottawa on horseback and inquired about Catholics in the area. Apparently finding things to his liking, Father Ponziglione offered Mass in Ottawa for the first time. After his departure, Father Ponziglione quickly made arrangements for a priest to serve the Catholics in town. In 1872, the Catholics in Ottawa attempted to erect a church of their own, but a severe storm destroyed the structure before it was complete, and the plans to build a church were abandoned. It wasn't until 1908 that the first Catholic church in Ottawa was built and given the name Sacred Heart. That church was destroyed by fire in 1913 when a faulty furnace exploded. Three months after the fire, the cornerstone for a new church was laid. This church too was destroyed by fire in 1940, as was the next church in 1979. The present Sacred Heart Church was built in 1980.

Church of the Ascension, Overland Park

As southern Overland Park continued to grow in the 1980s and 90s, the need for a new parish became evident. Thus, on July 14, 1991, Church of the Ascension was established with 200 registered families. Father Larry Albertson was its first pastor. By 1993, the parish had more than 1,000 registered families but no church. A church was completed in 1997, with seating for approximately 1,250 people. A school quickly followed, opening in September of that year.

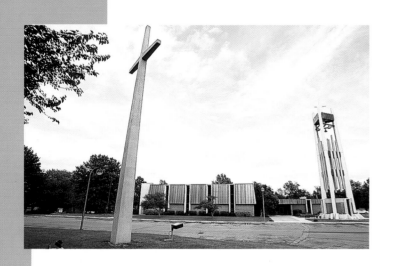

Park Mall and eventually moved to the Lenexa Community Center to keep up with the growing congregation. As the parish continued to grow, the need for a permanent facility became paramount. Despite the high cost of living at the time, the parish began construction on a combination church-school facility in 1983. It was completed the next year as the congregation approached 3,000 members.

Holy Cross, Overland Park

A new parish was established in Overland Park in 1968 with Father Robert Burger as its pastor. Holy Cross was voted as the name of the parish over St. Edward, Holy Spirit, and Precious Blood. Holy Cross has been described as a warm-hearted group of people of all ages, backgrounds and life experiences, brought together in the name of Jesus Christ. From its earliest days, when Mass was celebrated in the Glenwood Theater and CCD classes were taught in the Sunday-school rooms at Valley View Methodist Church, Holy Cross has played an active role in the community. Parishioners give generously, freely sharing their time, talent and treasures. They point with pride to the flourishing parish school and vibrant programs for religious education.

Holy Spirit, Overland Park

Holy Spirit Parish was established in 1981 with Father Robert Pflumm as its first pastor. Masses were first said in the theater at Oak

Queen of the Holy Rosary, Overland Park

Queen of the Holy Rosary Parish was established in 1944 after an archdiocesan study, done two years before, indicated that Overland Park was primed for rapid growth. Under the direction of Father John Ryan, the first pastor, the parish built a church (which won a national architectural award), a convent, a rectory and school. A huge mosaic of the Queen of the Holy Rosary on the church exterior honors the parish patron. Queen serves the spiritual needs of more than 1,500 families. The congregation is a blend of founding families, singles, and young families with children. Members of the Hispanic and Vietnamese communities add cultural diversity to parish life. The parish holds inter-faith prayer services with nearby churches, helps the homeless and those in financial need through various programs, and offers a wide variety of support groups for the widowed, bereaved, and returning Catholics. The parish school and school of religion enjoy the strong support of the parish. An elected parish council and the large number of programs offer parishioners the chance to assist in creating and maintaining spiritual development.

Holy Trinity, Paola

In 1858, six Irish families traveling from Indiana settled between Paola and Osawatomie. Upon learning of the settlers, Father Paul Ponziglione paid them a visit and celebrated Mass in one of their homes. In December of 1858, Father Ivo Schacht visited the settlement and took over its spiritual needs. Construction of a church in Paola began in 1858, but crop failures, drought, and the start of the Civil War halted the effort. The church was finally completed in 1865, but by 1877 it began to crumble. Faced with a deteriorating church, the parish started constructing a new one in 1880. In 1902 a school was built. The following year the Ursuline Sisters took charge of the school. On January 14, 1906, the church was destroyed by a fire of unknown origin. By the next year a new church had risen in its place. In 1959, the old school was replaced by a new one. In 1999, the parish completed a major renovation of the interior of the church.

Sacred Heart, Paxico

In 1870 a parish was established in Newbury and became a mission of Alma. In 1874, the Catholics of Newbury decided to build their own church. The first Mass was offered on November 29, 1874. In 1886, the town of Paxico was established one mile from Newbury along the railroad line, signaling the end of Newbury as a town for all practical purposes. In 1890, Father Joseph Hohe, pastor of Sacred Heart, started a Catholic school, which was staffed by Benedictine Sisters beginning in 1897. On January 7, 1921, the church was gutted by a fire. Only the walls were left standing. By the next year, a new, larger church was built. The church underwent major renovations in 1948 and 1969. The descendants of some of the founding families are still a part of the community. At the parish's 125th anniversary celebration in 1999, these descendants placed several historical items before the altar. The parish was, and continues to be an important part of the Paxico community.

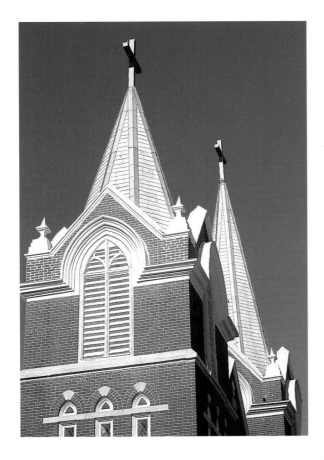

St. Theresa, Perry

Catholic activity in Perry began in 1880, when Father Francis Kraus visited local Catholics. Finding 20 Catholic families, Father Kraus raised the question of building a Catholic church in town, which he would care for. By 1884 a church had been built and named St. Cecilia. In 1903, a flood inundated Perry, but the church was spared

Ann. Construction on a church and school began in the spring of 1949. The school, which was completed before the church, opened on September 12, 1949, with 70 students and two Ursuline Sisters. The church was dedicated in November of that year. In 1964, a larger church with a seating capacity of 900 was built. It was dedicated in June, 1964.

St. Mary, Purcell

Catholicism in Purcell dates back to 1857, when Benedictine Father Henry Lemke cared for the spiritual needs of the settlers in the area. In 1959, Benedictine Father Edmunt Langenfelder organized nine families into a parish and celebrated Mass in their homes at irregular intervals. Later that year a church was constructed on 10 acres of land. It was cared for by the Benedictine Fathers. By 1877, the parish had grown to 250 members. The parish continued to grow, and in 1896 parishioners decided to build a

heavy damage. In 1918, a parish school was started and operated by the Benedictine Sisters. It would last only six years. In 1925, the cornerstone for a new church was laid, and the name was changed to St. Theresa. Education is an important part of St. Theresa Parish. In addition to religious education classes for students, the parish has offered a wealth of educational opportunities for adults on topics such as church history, sacraments, scripture, prayer and morality. The parish, which still boasts some of the families that helped build the original church in 1884, continues to cling to its rural heritage even as more and more families move into Perry, seeking to escape suburbia.

St. Ann, Prairie Village

From 1946 to 1948 the Catholic population in Prairie Village jumped from six to 80 families, prompting Bishop George Donnelly to establish a parish in the area. Father Patrick Fitzgerald was the first pastor of St.

new church, which was completed the following year. In 1906, the church was redecorated with new stations of the cross, statues and altar. An elementary school, staffed by Benedictine Sisters, was started in 1908. A high school was added in 1916 and operated until 1934. In 1960 the elementary school also closed. On August 7, 1991, a tornado hit the church steeple causing severe structural damage. Mass was celebrated in the parish hall until repairs could be made. The church was rededicated on March 21, 1992.

St. Therese, Richmond

The first drive to build a Catholic church in Richmond began in 1918 among a group of businessmen and retired farmers who believed a Catholic church would bring business to town. They decided that the Catholic families in Richmond, at that time numbering fewer than 20, would not be able to support the church, and so the matter was dropped for a time. Six years later, many of the same businessmen pleaded with the pastor of Scipio to ask his superiors to send a priest who could care for Richmond if a church were built. Although both the pastor and Bishop John Ward were hesitant, the bishop gave his consent for a church to be built in Richmond after at least half of the money to build the church had been raised. The church was completed by December, 1926. It has been under the care of Scipio's Carmelite community since its inception.

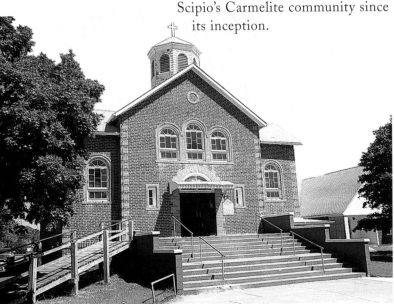

St. Agnes, Roeland Park

As the population began to increase in northeast Johnson County in the 1920s, Bishop John Ward sensed it was time to start a parish in the area. He established St. Agnes in 1923 and named Father James Ording its first pastor. The first church was completed on November 1, 1923. The chapel in the basement seated 260 people. The services of three Sisters of Loretto were secured to teach in the parish school. In 1927, a second story was added to the church and the chapel moved from the basement to the second floor, which had a seating capacity of 380. In 1929, the Ursulines took over the school. As the area continued to grow, the need for a new church was paramount. World War II slowed down much of the construction, but on Thanksgiving Day, 1943, the completed church was dedicated. In 1945 Father Herman Koch was made pastor of the parish by Bishop Paul Schulte and given instructions to establish a high school. That year, a freshman class started, marking the beginnings of Bishop Miege High School.

St. Stanislaus, Rossville

St. Stanislaus Parish began in 1899 as a mission of Immaculate Conception Parish in St. Marys. By the following year a church had been erected and dedicated. Though the parish struggled for much of its existence with low membership — usually fewer than 30 families — the 1980s saw the parish grow like never before. By 1982 the parish had 180 families. In 1997, the parish began construction on a religious education center and parish hall, which were finished in 1998. Plans have also been made to build a new church.

Sacred Heart, Sabetha

As early as 1879, the Catholics in Sabetha wanted a place of worship to call their own. Bishop Louis Fink finally gave them permission to build in 1883, and shortly thereafter a frame church was erected. A few years later, services at Sabetha were discontinued because of the small congregation. In 1920, Dr. Samuel Murdock donated a hospital in Sabetha to the Sisters of St. Joseph of Concordia, who took over its administration. Soon a small chapel was built for the Sisters, and a priest from Fidelity went to Sabetha to offer Mass. In 1921, Father A.J. Wasinger arrived in Sabetha and saw great potential for a church. Father Wasinger rallied the town's Catholics behind

the idea of building a new church. The church was dedicated in 1923. Although the parish struggled through the 30s, the 40s brought new growth to the area, and several improvements were made to the church. In 1990, the parish embarked on a fundraising effort for a new church. The groundbreaking for the new church was August 30, 1992, and the church was dedicated on October 10, 1993.

St. Mary, St. Benedict

St. Mary Parish was founded in 1859, more than a year before the Kansas Territory became a state. The first church was built in 1859 but quickly became too small and was replaced in 1864. The parish quickly outgrew that church also, building a new one in 1880. Nine years later, as the parish continued to grow rapidly, the parish contemplated building yet another church, one large enough to deal with all its future needs. On November 14, 1894, the bigger St. Mary Church was dedicated. The Roman-style church is listed on the National Register of Historic Places and is well-known for its exquisite interior. From 1980 to 1983, the church's interior underwent a major restoration as the paintings were cleaned and restored to their original excellence. The stained-glass windows were renovated between 1991 and 1994.

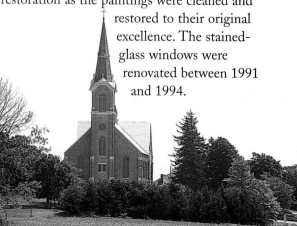

Immaculate Conception, St. Marys

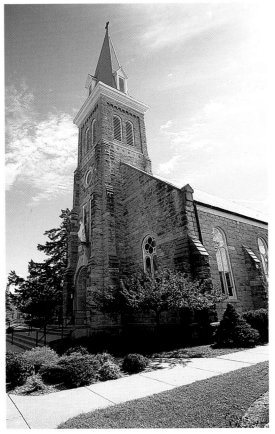

Members of the Potawatomi tribe at the Sugar Creek mission (near what is now Mound City) were forced westward in 1848 by the federal government. Their buildings were burned. The people eventually settled near what is now St. Marys. The Jesuit priests and Religious Sisters of the Sacred Heart followed the Potawatomi. A crude log-cabin church was quickly built in 1848 and dedicated to the Immaculate Conception. The following year a more permanent church was constructed. The Vicariate Apostolic of the Indian Territory was established in 1850, and Bishop John

Baptist Miege was chosen to head the territory in 1851. The newly consecrated Bishop John Baptist Miege made his way to St. Marys, and Immaculate Conception became his first cathedral. That lasted until 1855, when Bishop Miege moved his see to Leavenworth. In 1873, a larger church was built. That church was destroyed by fire in 1879. The present church was built in 1881. It was recently remodeled.

St. Boniface, Scipio

In 1858, Father Ivo Schacht arrived in Scipio to care for the German settlement that had settled along the creek. Work began on a church in September of that year and was finished in time for Christmas Mass. In 1864, two Carmelite priests arrived in Leavenworth and were given charge of St. Joseph Parish there. With a desperate need for priests, Father Louis Guenther, still a novice, was assigned to St. Boniface. With the construction of the railroad in Kansas, new life flowed into Scipio. In 1872 a larger church and a monastery were built. In 1873 Father Theodore Heimann, pastor of St. Boniface, started a college which proved short-lived. The construction of another new church began in 1881. In 1905 an artist improved the interior of the church. In 1919, the interior of the church was redecorated and the mysteries of the rosary were painted on the walls. In 1949, the church underwent an extensive renovation.

St. Patrick, Scranton

Catholics had settled in the area that is currently Scranton as far back as the 1850s, but it wasn't until Kansas became a state in 1868 that the first Mass was offered in the town. St. Patrick Parish was established in 1876, and soon thereafter a church was erected. The small frame structure served the parish until 1918 when a larger, Gothic-style church was built; it still stands today. In 1964, a gas line exploded causing considerable damage to the interior. In 1974, a severe storm swept through town shattering several stained-glass windows and causing much water damage. In 1976, the parish celebrated its centennial.

Sts. Peter and Paul, Seneca

Sts. Peter and Paul Parish got its start in 1869, when the Catholic families in town, numbering only 10, banded together to purchase an old public school building. The school was remodeled and Seneca had its first Catholic church, dedicated on July 11, 1869. With a Catholic church in town, and fertile land all around, Bishop Louis Fink promoted Seneca in Germany through advertisements. By the end of 1869, the original 10 families had grown to 80. In September, 1870, the parish started a school, with classes held in the church. In 1878 a school building was constructed and the services of the Benedictine Sisters were secured. In 1895 work began on a new church. When it was finished a new school building was started. Construction was complete in 1896. A

high school was started in 1911, operating until 1974. In 1994, the parish celebrated its 125th anniversary.

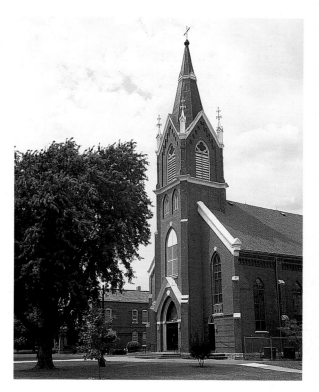

Good Shepherd, Shawnee

In 1972, Archbishop Ignatius Strecker invited the Capuchin priests to consider establishing a parish in the Shawnee-Lenexa area. Father Marvin Justi and Father Finian Meis answered the call and did a study of the area. Their conclusion was that the most urgent need for ministry was to the people in the many apartment complexes that had sprung up in the fast-growing area. Soon, small groups of 30

community. The Belgians were the focus of the 1998 services, while the Irish were the focus in 1999. Each Mass was celebrated in the respective group's native language, followed by activities highlighting the group's culture and traditions.

to 40 families were organized into mini-parishes, and Masses were celebrated in various apartment-complex clubhouses. This experimental approach was successful and the parish thrived. By the mid-1970s the parish had grown so large that the mini-parishes were no longer practical. A permanent church building was needed. On June 3, 1976, Good Shepherd Church was dedicated with space for as many as 900. In November of 1997, the parish broke ground on a new church as the number of families approached 1,500.

St. Joseph, Shawnee

In 1868, Father Anton Kuhls traveled to Shawnee from his parish in what is now Kansas City, Kansas, for a series of religious lectures. These lectures were a hit, and attendance steadily increased. It quickly became evident to Father Kuhls that a Catholic church in Shawnee could flourish. Father Kuhls oversaw the building of the church, which was completed in 1868. Today descendants of many of those early parishioners still grace St. Joseph. The parish encourages ecumenism in the Shawnee Christian community by helping to organize, promote and implement services involving area churches. Starting in 1998, the parish was instrumental in planning a community Palm Sunday service at Shawnee City Hall, where other congregations joined with St. Joseph. To celebrate Church Unity Week 1999, St. Joseph hosted a "Community of Love" concert with several area adult, children's, and bell choirs participating. Advent services focusing on ethnic groups began in 1997 with a focus on the Hispanic

Holy Family, Summerfield

The first church in Summerfield was built in 1892 by Father John Hurley for 21 families in the area. The parish was a mission of St. Bridget in Axtell until 1907, when it received its own pastor. During the pastorate of Father E. R. Embleau (1914-1923), a new Gothic-style church was built. In the early 1940s, a small fire broke out in the church causing considerable smoke damage. The whole interior had to be repainted. In 1989, with the proceeds saved from years of parish socials and picnics, the interior of the church was renovated.

116

Sacred Heart, Tonganoxie

Catholicism in Tonganoxie dates back to 1865, when missionary priests began offering Masses sporadically in private homes. In 1880, an old store building in Lawrence was moved just outside of Tonganoxie and converted into the town's first Catholic church. That church lasted 10 years until a new one was built. The first Mass in this new church was celebrated on January 26, 1890, even though the interior was not complete. It would be four years before the interior was finished. In 1908, the church was enlarged and other improvements were made. Improvements were also made to the church in the 1970s. In 1990, the parish celebrated its centennial.

Assumption, Topeka

Assumption is the oldest parish in Topeka, dating back to the mid-1800s, when it was served by Jesuit priests from Lawrence. The parish began to take shape in 1860, when Father Ivo Schacht, a priest from Lawrence, met with the Catholic property-owners of Topeka to discuss building a church. Father Schacht must have had some influence, because a church was under construction by 1861 and was completed the following year. In 1869, a parish school was started and staffed by the Sisters of Charity. As Topeka steadily grew, plans were made to build a larger church, which was completed in 1882. In 1911, Assumption started a high school. It was the beginning of what would become Hayden High School. On September 11, 1922, fire caused major damage in the church. On September 23, 1923, the cornerstone for the present Romanesque-style church was laid. Assumption is a culturally diverse parish with families that date back several generations. The parish participates in a program to provide daily sack lunches to the poor. Assumption also offers a daily noon Mass which brings into the church a number of Catholics working in the downtown area.

Christ the King, Topeka

Christ the King Parish was established in 1977 to meet the needs of the growing population in southwest Topeka. The parish started with 585 families. Father John Yadrich was named the first pastor. On July 20, 1980, Archbishop Ignatius Strecker blessed the newly constructed parish center and Masses moved there from Hayden High School. The parish broke ground on a church on July 29, 1984. The church, which has seating for 900, was dedicated on September 8, 1985. In 1995 the parish started a grade school. Christ the King is dedicated to providing food and clothing monthly for two local organizations, Let's Help and Doorstep. The parish has a strong ecumenical commitment, holding membership in Kansas Ecumenical Ministries and Interfaith of Topeka. The parish is also a member of Concerned Citizens

of Topeka, a group that addresses racism. For seven years Perpetual Adoration has taken place weekly in the parish chapel, involving close to 500 parishioners. Before the morning Mass, either a Rosary is offered for vocations, or, twice a week, the morning prayer of the Liturgy of the Hours is prayed.

Holy Name, Topeka

Holy Name Parish was established in the spring of 1914 by Bishop John Ward. Father J. A. Murphy, the first pastor, was asked by Bishop Ward to build a combination church-school. Construction on the facility began later that year. In 1915, Holy Name School opened, even though the school building was nowhere near completion. In 1916, a combination chapel-school was completed and dedicated. The chapel served as the parish church until an actual church building could be built. It was completed in 1925. During the summer of 1933, the interior of the church was frescoed, new stained-glass windows were placed, and the stations of the cross were hand-painted. A new school was built in 1941 and expanded in 1959. In 1985, the interior of the church underwent a major renovation.

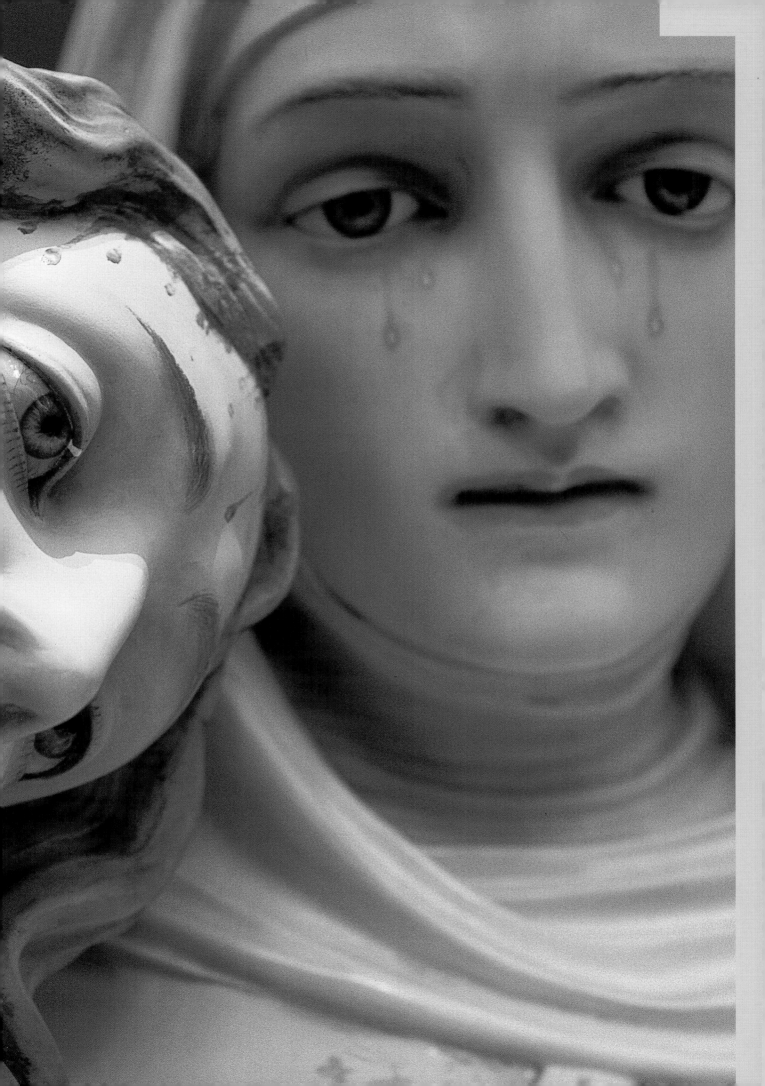

Most Pure Heart of Mary, Topeka

Most Pure Heart of Mary Parish was established in 1946 in southwest Topeka with 136 registered families. The first Mass was celebrated the following year in the basement chapel at St. Vincent Home in Topeka. In 1950, construction of a parish school began. A 600-seat chapel, built beneath the gymnasium, was completed in 1951. The first Mass in the new chapel was said on Thanksgiving Day. In 1958, plans were made to build a new church, which Archbishop Edward Hunkeler dedicated on April 16, 1961. The Gothic-style church seats more than 1,000 people.

Our Lady of Guadalupe, Topeka

At the beginning of the 20th century, approximately 20 Mexican families fleeing political unrest in their country arrived on the outskirts of Topeka. In 1914,

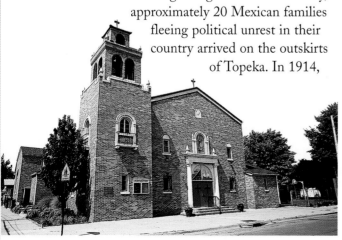

Pedro Lopez, a member of one of those families, recognized a priest from Mexico at the train station. Lopez struck up a conversation with the priest, Father Epifanio Ocampo, and expressed the desire of the Hispanic community to have its own parish. Father Ocampo decided to stay in town and the next day the two of them met with Father Francis Hayden, pastor of Assumption Parish in Topeka, to explain the Hispanics' plight. Father Hayden agreed that a Hispanic parish should be established. Soon thereafter, Our Lady of Guadalupe began celebrating Mass in a small store building. In 1921, the parish built a combination church-school. In 1933, the Fiesta Mexicana, a fundraiser for the school, began. The fiesta has grown into a much-anticipated, week-long event that brings the school much-needed revenue. A new church was built in 1950 and a new school in 1955.

Sacred Heart, Topeka

Sacred Heart Parish was established in 1919 with Father George Eckart as its first pastor. The following year a temporary chapel was erected as work began on a parish facility. Sacred Heart Church and school were dedicated on May 30, 1921. In 1935, the church was remodeled. In 1936, the building's boiler exploded, blowing out the church's stained-glass windows and splintering many of its doors. In 1944, the church underwent a major renovation and redecoration. In 1951, a flood swept through Topeka causing minor damage to the church. In 1966, the parish began construction of a new contemporary church. It was dedicated the following year.

people abandoned the city for the suburbs. The flood of 1951, which destroyed many homes, also resulted in a population decrease which affected the parish membership. In 1970, the parish school closed because of decreasing enrollment.

St. Joseph, Topeka

In 1886, Bishop Louis Fink asked the recently ordained Father Francis Henry to organize a German parish in Topeka. The first Mass was celebrated February 13, 1887, in Assumption Church. Later that year, a simple two-story building that served as both a church and school was built. In 1900, a new church was built, followed by a new school in 1912. In 1909, the services of the Sisters of Charity were secured for the school. The 1950s were a difficult time for St. Joseph as more and more

St. Matthew, Topeka

St. Matthew Parish was established in 1955 with Father Arthur Trompeter as its first pastor. Mass was celebrated at the Army Reserve Armory until a church was completed in 1958. In September of that year, the parish school opened with 245 students; it was staffed by the Benedictine Sisters. In 1965, enrollment had grown so large that an addition had to be made to the school building. In 1974, the church was renovated. It was rededicated on March 17, 1974. In 1978, a kindergarten was added to the

The first Mass celebrated in the church was in May, 1881. The church was simple with nothing more than a temporary confessional and a makeshift altar. There were no pews. In 1900, a belfry was added to the front of the church. In the late 1920s, there was much discussion about building a larger church, but in the end the parish decided to enlarge and remodel the old one. The newly remodeled church was dedicated on April 15, 1931. In the late 1950s, Benedictine Father Egbert Hall, pastor of St. Charles, started making plans for a new church. He also wanted to start a school. Ground was broken for a new church and a school on August 19, 1962. The facility was finished the following year.

school. In 1987, St. Matthew Parish moved into a new, modern church building with seating for 800. It was dedicated on August 30, 1987.

St. Charles, Troy

There has been a Catholic presence in Troy since 1862, when Benedictine Father Thomas Bartl would look in on the Catholics of the area on his way to various missions. Nearly 20 years later the community built its first church.

Immaculate Conception, Valley Falls

A parish in Valley Falls was organized in 1858. Masses were celebrated in private homes until 1872, when a small brick church was built. By 1907, the church was too small and a larger, Gothic-style church was erected. In 1908, the parish started a school in the old church and secured the teachings services of the Benedictine Sisters. In 1924 the church was torched by the Ku Klux Klan and destroyed. A new Roman-style church was dedicated on Thanksgiving Day, 1926. In 1968, the parish school was closed because of a shortage of teaching Sisters. Over the years the laity, especially the Altar Society and the Knights of Columbus, have played an important role in the growth of the church by dedicating their time and skills to enhance the parish.

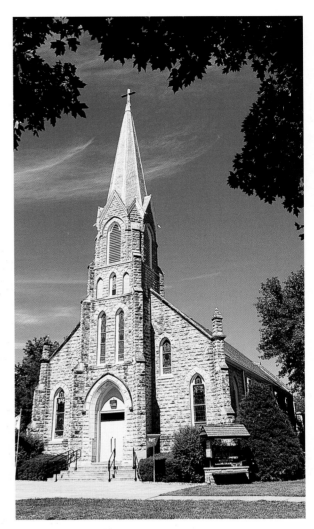

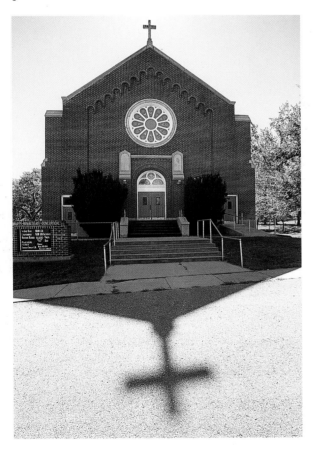

St. Bernard, Wamego

In the early 1870s, the Catholics in Wamego began to make noise about building a church in town but, because of financial difficulties, never saw the project through to fruition. In 1879, Father Bernard Nuttman took over the pastoral service to Wamego Catholics and encouraged them to continue with their plans to build the church. By the following year a church had been built. In 1906, the church was badly damaged by fire. Although the church was salvaged and repaired, the parish decided to go forward with building a new church, using the old one as a parish hall. This new church, Gothic in design, was dedicated March 3, 1908. In 1923, a parish school was opened. In the early 1970s the school closed. The parish currently offers perpetual adoration and is active in the Wamego Community Council of Churches which, among other things, includes ecumenical Good Friday and Thanksgiving services.

St. Monica, Waterville

Catholicism in Waterville dates back to 1866, when the first Mass was said in private homes, but it wasn't until 1910 that a church was built. On May 2, 1911, Bishop John Ward dedicated the church. In the 1920s, the church was badly damaged by fire, but not destroyed. When the church was repaired a bell tower was added.

St. Joseph, Wathena

The first church in Wathena was built in 1869. In 1880, a parish school was started and staffed by the Benedictine Sisters. As the community grew, the old church became inadequate and a new one was needed.

Ground was broken for this new church in the spring of 1913; it was finished the following year. The first Mass was celebrated on February 22, 1914. The old church was converted into a school. In 1949, ground was broken

for a new school building, which was dedicated on September 4, 1950. The school closed in 1970 for financial reasons.

St. Joseph, Waverly

In 1886, Father Joseph Walsh, pastor of St. Patrick Parish, Emerald, organized the scattered Catholics around Waverly into a parish. With a parish organized, its members immediately took to building a church. In 1899, Father A. J. Doman was appointed pastor of St. Joseph; he remained until 1908. During his pastorate he renovated the original church's interior and exterior. In 1915, the church was again renovated and a bell tower and steeple were added.

Holy Rosary, Wea

The first Holy Rosary church was erected in 1869. Father Sebastian Favre traveled on horseback from Lawrence to offer Mass to the early settlers of Wea. Between 1895 and 1896, a larger, brick church was constructed to keep up with the growing population in the area, and a school was started. That church was destroyed on April 9, 1905, when lightning struck it. Construction of a new church began immediately and was near completion when a cyclone leveled the unfinished structure on September 14, 1905. Discouraged, but not beaten, the parish geared up to rebuild once again. On May 29, 1906, a new church was dedicated by Bishop Thomas Lillis. In 1970, the parish school closed because of financial difficulties.

St. Teresa supported a parish school, which Benedictine Sisters staffed, from 1885 to 1970. The current church was built in 1966. Many families in Westphalia can trace their roots back to these early settlers. Westphalia is a strong Catholic community comprised of people who believe in working together and helping one another. The Altar Society serves lunch for bereaved families after the funerals of their loved ones. The Knights of Columbus sponsors work days to help older citizens of the town with repair work and property cleanup. In addition, those who find themselves in difficult situations know they can always look to the Catholic community.

St. Teresa, Westphalia

The first Mass in Westphalia was celebrated in a private home on April 13, 1881, just a year after the town was established by German settlers who brought with them a strong Catholic tradition.

St. James, Wetmore

Missionary priests cared for the spiritual needs of Catholics in Wetmore as far back as 1865, but it wasn't until Father John Begley arrived on the scene in 1879 that the first church was constructed. For most of its history, St. James has been a mission parish. In 1938, Father Angelus Lingenfelser, OSB, became pastor of St. James, and was instrumental in starting a parish school and obtaining a building to go along with it. By 1960 the school had outgrown its old one-room building and a new school was built. The school closed in 1969, and the school building was remodeled into the present church.

BIBLIOGRAPHY

Beckman, Peter, OSB, *The Catholic Church on the Kansas Frontier 1850-1877* (The Catholic University of America, 1943).

Beckman, Peter, OSB, Kansas Monks: *A History of St. Benedict's Abbey* (Benedictine College Press, Atchison, Kansas, 1957).

Buckner, Sister Mary, SCL, *History of The Sisters of Charity of Leavenworth, Kansas* (Hudson-Kimberly Publishing Co., Kansas City, Mo., 1889).

Callan, Louise, RSCJ, Philippine Duchesne: *Frontier Missionary of the Sacred Heart 1769-1852* (The Newman Press, Westminster, Maryland, 1957).

Garraghan, Gilbert J., S.J., Ph.D., *The Jesuits of the Middle United States,* Vols. I and II (America Press, New York, 1938).

Kinsella, T. H., LL.D., *The History of Our Cradle Land* (Casey Printing Co., Kansas City, 1921).

Mooney, Catherine M., RSCJ, Philippine Duchesne: *A Woman with the Poor* (Paulist Press, New York/Mahwah, N.J., 1990).

Muller, Herman J., SJ, Bishop East of the Rockies: *The Life and Letters of John Baptist Miege, S.J.* (Loyola University Press, Chicago, Illinois, 1994).

Everett Rich, *The Heritage of Kansas* (Flint Hills Book Co., 1964).

Rothensteiner, Rev. John, *History of the Archdiocese of St. Louis* (Blackwell Wielandy Co., St. Louis, Mo., 1928).

Strecker, Archbishop I. J. *The Church in Kansas, 1850-1905: A Family Story* (Forest of Peace Publishing, Leavenworth, 1999).